Papers, Papers, Papers

Papers, Papers, Papers

An English Teacher's Survival Guide

Carol Jago

HEINEMANN
Portsmouth, NH

Heinemann
A division of Reed Elsevier Inc.
361 Hanover Street
Portsmouth, NH 03801–3912
www.heinemann.com

Offices and agents throughout the world

The author and publisher wish to thank those who have generously given permission to reprint borrowed materials:

American Diploma Project benchmarks reprinted by permission of Achieve, Inc.

Excerpt from *Hold Online Essay Scoring* copyright © by Holt, Rinehart, and Winston. All rights reserved. Reprinted by permission of the publisher.

Library of Congress Cataloging-in-Publication Data
Jago, Carol, 1951–
   Papers, papers, papers : an English teacher's survival guide / Carol Jago.
     p. cm.
   Includes bibliographical references.
   ISBN 0-325-00828-0 (alk. paper)
   1. English language—Composition and exercises—Study and teaching (Secondary)—United States—Handbooks, manuals, etc. 2. English teachers—Workload—United States—Handbooks, manuals, etc. 3. Grading and marking (students)—United States—Handbooks, manuals, etc. I. Title.

LB1631.J364 2005
808'.042'0712—dc22
                            2005006714

Editor: Lisa Luedeke
Production: Elizabeth Valway
Cover design: Night & Day Design
Composition: House of Equations, Inc.
Manufacturing: Louise Richardson

Printed in the United States of America on acid-free paper

09 08 07 06   RRD   2 3 4 5

To my colleagues at Santa Monica High School, the most professional group of teachers I have ever known. Their determination to do their best for students continues to inspire me and to force me to question my practice. They also help me laugh.

Contents

Contents

Introduction:
Don't Let the Papers Get You Down

Wherever we English teachers gather, we complain about grading papers. Although teachers are reading as fast as they can, the pile of unread essays just seems to grow taller. Guilt mounts. Warning signs gather. We start fantasizing about accidentally leaving a stack of papers atop the car and losing them to the wind. We consider driving to the Pacific and consigning the pile to the ocean. We look with envy at colleagues teaching music and art and wonder how far our teaching credentials might stretch. We ask a recently retired English teacher how she is doing, only to hear, "I don't miss the papers!" We think about changing careers. This book is designed to keep teachers from doing that by suggesting ways to manage the paper load.

We can't quit. The work is too important. The National Commission on Writing in America's Schools and Colleges' report *The Neglected "R"* affirms the essential role that writing plays in a child's education. The report boldly proclaims, "Writing today is not a frill for the few, but an essential skill for the many" (2003, 2). Students who don't write well founder when they go to college and struggle on the job, forever hiding their poor composition skills. English teachers know that writing is vital for our students' prospects. That is why we martyr ourselves reading their essays. I know one newly-wed who would rise at 4:00 AM and sneak into the bathroom of her tiny apartment to grade papers while her husband slept. A first-year teacher in my department was at school until 9:00 PM for an entire week, buried in student essays.

One way to lessen the burden would be for teachers in other disciplines to assign more writing and thus relieve English teachers from bearing full responsibility for teaching composition. *The Neglected "R"* specifically recommends that writing be assigned across the curriculum. The authors insist that "Writing is everybody's business, and state and local curriculum guidelines should require writing in every curriculum area and at all grade levels" (5). I have been saying this for so long that I feel like Cassandra, fated to speak the truth but never to be heeded. In order to avoid developing a deep resentment toward those with whom I work every day, I have given up. With the exception of Advanced Placement History, few content area classes consider writing vitally important in their curriculum. I wish it were otherwise, but English teachers are in this alone. That said, we must not allow it to become the case that only teachers without families or a life outside the classroom are able to teach children to write well. It should not be necessary to sacrifice every evening and all day Sunday to the grind of grading papers. Ours cannot become a system where only heroes or martyrs have the moral fiber to succeed.

For the past thirty years I have taught English in a comprehensive public high school. Class size in California is some of the largest in the country. I have 36 to 38 students in every class. They write essays every four weeks. I estimate that I have graded 44,000 essays. Just doing the sums makes me tired. Actually, I like reading student papers . . . the first ten. It's the next twenty-six that get me down. This book offers methods I developed for moving through a stack of papers efficiently and, I believe, accurately. They do not always represent paragon pedagogy. If I had twenty or fewer students in a class I would do many things differently. As things stand, I do the best that I can. Many of the ideas I garner from workshops or books about writing instruction sound wonderful *prima facie* but prove impractical for a teacher who meets 150 students a day. A website offering advice to college instructors suggested reading the student paper once very quickly for a sense of the grade and then a second time to comment. While this method may be valuable for student writers, the cost in terms of wear and tear on me is great. I read papers once.

You may find that some of what I suggest doesn't work for you or needs certain adjustments for your students. Feel free to tweak. I never seem to complete any lesson in exactly the manner I executed it the year before. You may employ other strategies for keeping to a minimum the number of papers you collect and wonder why I don't include them here: for example, group writing assignments. This process, where four students collaborate on a single essay, has been enthusiastically explained to me many times, but I remain unconvinced. Writing should be a solitary act. Many teachers use a list of symbols to simplify their markings on student essays. If such a list works for you, use it. I don't include samples of such codes because they seem to add one more layer of insulation between the teacher and the student. Maybe I'm just constitutionally averse to codes. What you have in your hands is not the definitive Way to Grade Papers but one teacher's methods—practices that have served me well.

The belief that all students—whatever the funding formula for student-teacher ratios in their state—deserve sound writing instruction is the precept that keeps me going, and keeps me grading. If I quit teaching English, driven out by the guilt that I'm not meeting with students for writing conferences on every draft or that I fail to catch every comma splice, then children will be further shortchanged. We owe it our students not to let the paper load defeat us.

Papers, Papers, Papers

ONE

Comment Rather Than Correct

Correcting student papers and commenting on them are different exercises. Yet it is an occupational hazard to confuse them. This inevitably is the reason for the reluctance of teachers in other subject areas to assign essays. Many content area teachers are secretly afraid they won't catch all grammatical and syntactical errors and will, as a result, appear incompetent to students and parents. English teachers, on the other hand, too often take disproportionate pride in their eagle eye for indeterminate pronoun references and dangling participles and, consequently, sometimes expend more time than the student on perfecting the paper. This is an absurd outcome borne of the finest motives. Although certain obsessive-compulsive behaviors are compatible with good teaching—organization, tidiness, a comfort with repetition—it is neither necessary nor desirable for English teachers to rewrite a student's paper between the lines.

Student writers barely glance at such rewritten student papers; the prospect of yet more detailed critical work causes them to quickly toss the paper into the trash on the way out of class. Destroying the evidence, the student imagines, will make the bad news go away. If you feel you must identify every mistake, make sure you invest your effort on a student's draft rather than on the final copy. Be aware, however, that students can be so overwhelmed by the number of corrections suggested to a draft that many errors will be repeated in the revised paper. Absorbing and correcting the minutiae of textual criticism is too demanding a task.

Clearly some mistakes in grammar and usage should be identified whenever and wherever we spot them:

- subject-verb agreement
- spelling
- run-on sentences and fragments
- there/their/they're
- its/it's
- capitalization

I find I can circle and fix such errors almost automatically, leaving the rest of my attention for the paper's content. Rewriting students' garbled sentences in clearer prose demands a different kind of focus. When I try to revise for the student I must invest more of my time. It's also exhausting because I'm doing the students' work for them. This is not the best use of my time. I already know how to write.

We use the terms *correcting papers*, *grading papers*, and *reading essays* interchangeably. Distinguishing the separate tasks involved in reading a student paper can provide insight into the process. On one level we identify and correct student errors in grammar and usage. On a second level we rephrase and revise sentences for improved clarity and style. On a third level we comment on content and respond to a student's expressed ideas. Grading papers is so exhausting because we operate on all three levels at once.

Level 1: Identify Mechanical Errors

I used to underestimate the importance of mechanical correctness in first drafts and other informal student writing and would encourage students to "freewrite" without concern for anything but putting ideas down on paper. It now seems to me that this method did more harm than good. A few students did seem to enjoy the chance to focus on content but often what they produced was unreadable. I am increasingly convinced that students should not put off making subjects agree with verbs or spelling common words correctly until the editing stage. They need to capitalize proper nouns every time they put pen to paper or fingers to keyboard. They should place apostrophes between the proper letters in a contraction every time they write one. Practice doesn't make perfect when students are continually repeating their mistakes. It legitimizes and ingrains error. Those who promote freewriting probably don't work with high school students who commonly mistake "were" for "where" or "could of" for "could have." With many of my students it is not a momentary lapse of attention to detail that causes these errors but rather years of practice in making them without correction.

I worry that we encourage carelessness when we tell students, "Don't worry about spelling or commas. Just write." Would a piano teacher suggest that a novice stop paying attention to the notes? Would a soccer coach yell to his midfielders, "Don't worry about technique. Just play"? I think not. Both know that accomplished performance depends on a muscle memory of accuracy that comes from constant practice. The next time students ask if spelling counts, tell them "Yes!" You will be telling the truth whether or not you figure correctness into the grade. Correctness counts in profound ways. If students' use of language is inexact and their prose is full of errors, their ideas will be too easily discounted. Correctness will count not only in their polished final drafts but also in the email messages they'll send and the correspondence they compose in the workplace.

While it is good teaching practice to recommend that students get their big ideas down on paper without worrying about precise word choice or varied sentence structures, it is certainly not good practice to encourage students to abandon or discount basic skills. The habit of correctness needs to become automatic so that writing can proceed without focusing much attention on spelling, capitalization, or common punctuation. One can hope that the attention most states' language arts standards have drawn to usage, mechanics, and grammar throughout elementary school will—over time—make a difference, but I'm not holding my breath. Too many students always seem to fall between the cracks.

Dear Mrs. Jago,
I learned alot in this class. this class made me use parts of my mind that I didnt really use before. I also liked most of the assignments we had. I just hope I pass this class to graduate. I love being in your class. I wouldn't change it for nothing.

Sincerely,
Jorge C.

Jorge is seventeen years old and the product of thirteen years of public education. The note appears exactly as he wrote it. If this isn't evidence of malpractice, including my own, I don't know what is. Generations of students are passing through our schools without having acquired the rudiments of correct usage. It is small wonder that so many college freshmen need remedial English classes and no wonder that their employers are less than satisfied with the preparatory work that teachers have performed.

I can offer plenty of excuses: There were thirty-nine students in Jorge's senior English class. I can point to his spotty attendance or casual attitude toward academics. If I really want to delude myself I could blame Jorge's lack of skills on the fact that he speaks Spanish at home or that his family is poor. The no-fault truth is that Jorge has been shortchanged. He came to the public schools for an education, and we have allowed him, even encouraged him, to graduate with writing skills no reasonable person would tolerate from a sixth grader. The desire to improve education for students like Jorge animated legislators from both sides of the House to support the No Child Left Behind legislation. The same desire keeps public school teachers toiling under almost impossible circumstances. We need to work with students as they come to us; we are obliged to help them write with correct spelling, usage, and grammar.

This means that, when we grade papers, we must ensure that a student essay rife with errors is returned with those errors clearly identified. The paper should bleed. Before you call me heartless and consign this book to the shelf for reactionary philosophy, let me assure you that I wield my red pen with love. I care so much about these teenagers who are making elementary errors that I want them to stop NOW. Red helps me send that message.

4

Color psychologist Leatrice Eiseman, director of the Pantone Color Institute in Carlstadt, New Jersey, and author of five books on color believes that teachers should replace the red ink with purple to "soften the blow of red. Red is a bit over-the-top in its aggression" (Oaki 2004). In an interview for *The Boston Globe* she explained that as a mix of red and blue, the color purple embodies red's sense of authority but also blue's association with serenity, making it a less negative and more constructive color for correcting student papers. She feels that, because the color is linked to creativity and royalty, it is more encouraging to students.

When I was interviewed for this same article I told reporter Naomi Aoki that despite Ms. Eiseman's expert advice, I had no intention of switching to purple, or green, or any other color for marking student papers. I told her that every time I collect a set of student papers I treat myself to a new red pen. Fortunately she left this detail out of her article. I need the power of red to help me send students the message that their mistakes are serious and be treated accordingly. Students will be judged by their correctness as much as by the power of their ideas. I want them to see clearly how those ideas are currently obscured by error. I will tell some students that I can't begin to comment on their content until they correct the mechanical errors. For others, I have to assign a D to focus their attention. Still others need reassurance that their ideas are excellent and their insights so remarkable that they deserve much better than this shabby presentation. You know your students. You must be the judge.

Marking mechanical errors in student papers can become an almost-automatic reflex. Don't worry if you miss one or two; just make sure the "look" of the graded paper reflects the extent of the mechanical errors committed. You will not have to spend extra time in purgatory for overlooking the odd misplaced modifier. Do students become so discouraged by bleeding essays that they give up? Not if you let them know that your red marks are not a judgment of them or their ideas but of the piece of work at hand.

An effective but time-consuming way to deal with mechanical errors is to type up sentences from student papers and have the class correct the mistakes. Dana Danesi, an extraordinary first-year teacher at my school, prepared a three-page worksheet after correcting a set of ninth-grade students' returned essays. She duplicated a long list of error-ridden sentences and spent a class period going over ways to correct them.

Spot the Grammatical Error

1. He sees that his mother might of gone through the same difficulties in life that he has experienced, that she may not of shown emotions or pity.
2. If they would've face what they were afraid of, they would've been able to spare a boy's life.
3. In conclusion we can see that through the many relationships in this book weather a person is rich or poor high ranking on the social ladder of low ones morals and beliefs play have no connection to their social rankings.
4. The author shows that even though it may looks as though you are in between a rock and a hard spot there is always a way to accomplish your goals.

While this is clearly more authentic practice than simply turning to a page in a grammar book to work on mechanical correctness, I don't think it is realistic to expect teachers to take an extra hour to prepare such one-time-use lessons. I am sad to report that this wonderful young teacher is applying to a master's program in counseling for next year. Could it be the paper load that has her looking for alternatives to teaching English?

Level 2: Rephrase for Clarity and Style

Level 2 corrections are all-consuming. Circling spelling errors is vastly superior and more rapidly performed than straightening out awkward sentence structures. My solution? Don't straighten them out yourself. That is not your function—or not your function at this point. Instead of rewriting students' sentences for them, underline these syntactical nightmares and write in the margin one of the following comments:

"This sentence doesn't make sense as written."

"You have lost me here."

"What exactly do you mean by this?"

"Can you rephrase this more clearly?"

"Help!"

By responding like a reader who is trying to understand what the student has written you send the message that the passage needs revision without doing the revising yourself. Such rewriting of student prose is particularly futile when students are not going to be required to submit another draft. Hours of teacher time are invested with little payoff in terms of student learning. At some point we need to launch the student on the voyage of nondependent writing.

A more effective technique for helping students grapple with awkward or imprecise sentences is to have them focus on individual sentences that need work. When you return graded papers, put students into small groups and have them each choose a sentence from their papers that has been identified as lacking in clarity. By highlighting with a yellow marker one particular sentence in each paper you will help them get down to business quickly. The writer reads the sentence aloud to the group. The group discusses what needs fixing. The following is a transcript from one such session. Students agreed to have a tape recorder in their midst but soon forgot its presence. The "she" referred to in their conversation is, of course, me, their teacher. The sentence came from an essay written to this prompt: Analyze how Reuven and Danny, characters in Chaim Potok's novel *The Chosen*, were in their lives chosen. Consider exploring what it means to be chosen and how each of the boys felt about being chosen.

> *Ian:* OK, I'll go first and get it over with. My sentence that she highlighted was "Being chosen is just when you get the feeling like now they picked me."
>
> *Maggie:* Read it again. The end sounds funny.
>
> *Ian:* Here, you look at it.

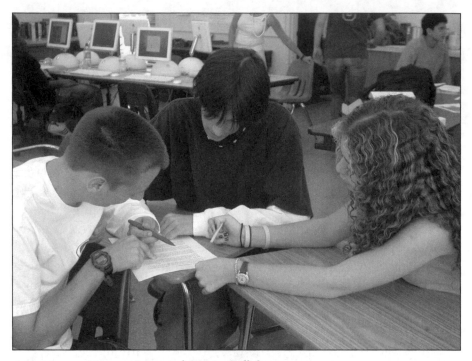

FIGURE 1–1   *Trevor, Ian, and Kimia Collaborate*

Kimia: "Being chosen is just when you get the feeling like now they picked me." I think the end sounds like a quote or something. It doesn't fit with the beginning of the sentence.

Trevor: I'll bet she hated the "is just when" part. Didn't she tell us not to write "is when"?

Ian: So what am I supposed to do?

Kimia: What did you want to say?

Ian: I was trying to say that being chosen is like being picked for a team. It's a good feeling but kinda scary, too.

Trevor: I say start over.

Ian: She said to fix this one.

Trevor: But if it doesn't say what you mean, what good is it?

Kimia: Why don't you take what you just said, "Being chosen for Danny and Reuven was both something and something."

Ian: Something, something?

Kimia: Fill in the blanks.

Trevor: What about "Danny and Reuven felt special to have been chosen but worried about what this would mean"?

Mrs. Jago (*circulating to their group*): There's a word for this feeling. It's *ambivalent.*

Ian: That's cool, but we're done with me. It's Kimia's turn.

Consider the difference between this lesson and a scenario wherein you revise every awkward student sentence. Students are practicing writing clear sentences. They are talking about how to improve syntax. When you do all the revision, you are the only person becoming a better writer. Also consider that the lesson I've just described does not require you to type up student sentences, wait in line at the copier, or otherwise do more work. Teachers cannot work any harder. We have to be more effective in using time and resources.

I know of no evidence that teachers rewriting student papers results in improved student writing. We do it because we can't help ourselves. It allows us to feel virtuous about a job well done. If it means we spent 115 minutes revising a single paper, it may also mean that we are considering quitting teaching or assigning fewer student essays.

Level 3: Comment on Content

Even more than overwork, it is a sense of futility that overwhelms writing teachers. We chose this profession in the hope of making a difference, valuing significance in our work over financial success or power. We garner satisfaction from knowing our students are learning. Nothing depresses us more than the feeling that no matter how hard we teach, students aren't improving. No matter how many papers we collect and grade, the essays remain unfocused and dull. In order to make tangible growth as writers, students need personalized feedback.

Boilerplate comments like "Needs work," "Well done!" and "Lacks clarity" are not enough. Teachers need to comment on content.

I handle this commentary by writing a formal letter to the student, addressing the writer by name and beginning with a positive statement. Then, without recourse to a "however" or "but" proceed to suggest ways the student could improve the essay. Often I close with a personal comment cheering the student on or assuring him or her that I am here to help. Here are some examples of the kind of notes I write.

On an analytical essay about Ernest Gaines' *A Lesson Before Dying* by a tenth grader who is a strong reader but weak writer:

Dear Sam,
Your essay exudes an enthusiasm for Gaines' story that is infectious. Be careful not to allow your strong feelings for the book turn what should be an analytical essay—remember the key prompt verb: ANALYZE—into an evaluation of the novel. This shouldn't be a book review but an analysis of the irony; implicit in the teacher being the one who learns a "lesson." Thanks so much for being such a terrific leader in your literature circle. You really helped your group understand what they read.

Mrs. J

You will notice that my note, while friendly, employs academic language (infectious, evaluation, implicit). I rejoice when a student approaches me about the meaning of a word in my note. Using such vocabulary both frees me from translating my thoughts into baby talk and helps students become familiar with the language of writing instruction.

This language of writing instruction is widely agreed upon. The Praxis II Teacher Licensure Exam for English Language, Literature, and Composition: Pedagogy requires candidates to answer questions about a student's writing sample. Some of these questions ask about strengths, weaknesses, and errors in the conventions of Standard written English. You can find models of excellent, adequate, and inadequate teacher responses at www.ets.org/praxis/prxtest.html#sasat. Areas that show strengths and weaknesses in student papers include:

- essay organization
- paragraph organization
- quality of descriptive detail
- sentence variety and complexity
- sense of audience
- sense of voice

Errors in the conventions of Standard written English include:

- sentence fragments
- run-on sentences
- subject-verb agreement errors
- verb tense inconsistency
- pronoun-antecedent agreement errors
- nonparallel construction
- dangling or misplaced modifiers
- misplaced semicolons or commas

Praxis guidelines suggest that an effective teacher response to a student essay:

1. gives the student a thoughtful description of one or two major strengths and weaknesses;
2. describes a highly effective strategy for revising;
3. is clear, coherent, and well organized throughout;
4. has a positive and supportive tone;
5. clearly displays facility with language, syntax, and the conventions of Standard English; and
6. is about 350–400 words long.

I know I don't often write 350–400 words back to students. On average such communications contain 50–100 words. My response to Sam was 86 words long. I wonder how many students Praxis guidelines authors meet every day. This is not to say the Praxis is wrong, only that class size in California makes point number 6 unrealistic. If I spent twenty minutes on each of the seventy-six essays I will be collecting tomorrow from two sophomore English classes, it would take twenty-five hours of reading time to finish the stack. Given that my senior English classes will be turning in essays in a week's time, something has to give. My solution? Read fast. Write fast. I aim for seven to eight minutes per paper.

Although my notes to students are personalized, I am working from a stock of previously written comments stored in my head. Students tend to need similar urgings and instructions. For a student whose essay is relatively well written but didn't address the prompt well, I write:

> Dear Rebecca,
> You have insightful things to say about the weather as a metaphor for the author's attitudes. I've never thought about the sun's rays in this fashion before. Focus more specifically on the prompt next time. The essay would be clearer if your first sentence directly answered the question raised in the prompt. It would then be easier for a reader to follow the logic of your supporting evidence. You are such an excellent reader that I'm keen to see your writing skills match your reading skills.
>
> Mrs. J

This for an unpersuasive persuasive essay:

> Dear Tyler,
> No reader of your essay can doubt the strength of your passion for students' right to wear what they like to school. You have forgotten, though, to include concessions to the opposition. Why would someone think that uniforms are a good idea? Your essay is full of energetic assertions but little evidence to support your claims. A key anecdote could really help to make your case more effectively. Even though I disagree with your thesis, I want your argument to succeed!
>
> Mrs. J

And this for an essay that is hardly an essay at all—one of those three-hundred-word submissions in 28-point font with extra lines skipped between paragraphs:

Dear Audra,

Intriguing title and introduction. You make me want more—much, much more. Fulfilling the demands of this assignment requires an essay that is at least twice as long as what you have written here. It's not that longer is always better but without development your essay is incomplete. Next time be sure to include concrete examples to support your thesis. Please come see me if you want help generating ideas for supporting evidence.

Mrs. J

I believe students are more likely to read such personal notes than coded teacher responses. I hope they are less likely to be ignored. It is not enough for a writing teacher to be "right" about what is wrong in a student paper. To be effective we also need to be heard and be heeded. When we are effective, student writing improves. When student writing improves, we experience the satisfaction of a good day's work.

Rainer Maria Rilke responded to Franz Kappus' request for feedback on his writing with this advice:

> You ask whether your verses are good. You ask me. You have asked others before. You send them to magazines. You compare them with other poems. You have asked others before. You send them to magazines. You compare them with other poems, and you are disturbed when certain editors reject your efforts. Now (since you have allowed me to advise you) I beg you to give up all that. You are looking outward, and that above all you should not do now. Nobody can counsel and help you, nobody. There is only one single way. Go into yourself. Search for the reason that bids you write; find out whether it is spreading out its roots in the deepest places of your heart, acknowledge to yourself whether it is spreading out its roots in the deepest places of your heart, acknowledge to yourself whether you would have to die if it were denied you to write. This above all—ask yourself in the stillest hour of your night: *must* I write? (1962, 18–19)

While Rilke urges the young poet to consider what it means to be compelled from within to write, our students are compelled from without. They ignore our chiding and corrections at their peril. At the same time, like Rilke, I try to appeal to what is noblest in my students' natures. If they are to write well they must develop their own radar for knowing when what they write matches what is expected.

TWO

Using Scoring Guides and Rubrics

One of the most significant developments in writing instruction over the past twenty years has been the increased use of scoring guides for assessing student writing. In the bad old days teachers simply assigned and evaluated writing, giving grades according to an inner sense that students were expected to intuit and accept without question. Rubrics help to clarify grading process. While there will always be discrepancies among teachers however well "normed" they might be, adherence to a common scoring guide across a department—and ideally throughout a school—can bring consistency to what from a student's perspective is a somewhat idiosyncratic process.

Having clear expectations helps improve student performance, and when students write better the job of correcting papers becomes less onerous. The time you invest working through rubrics with students before they write, offering model papers during the process, and having students judge their own work with respect to agreed-upon standards should reduce the amount of time you need to spend with red pen in hand later. Coherent writing instruction makes a difference.

While there are many sample rubrics that schools can adopt, the construction of a scoring guide of your own builds consensus among department members. Instead of collectively grumbling about what students can't do, you find yourselves talking about the features that make up excellent student writing. As you go into committee to deliberate on these features, many differences of opinion get aired. You begin to build consensus. Constructing a department-wide scoring guide at Santa Monica High School also forced teachers to look more closely at what was being expected of our students at a state level. In order to graduate, California students must past an exit exam that includes a writing sample. One of the types of writing required is response to literature. Student "responses" must:

- be analytical
- exhibit careful reading and insight in their interpretations
- connect the student's own responses to the writer's techniques and to specific textual references
- draw supported inferences about the effects of a literary work on its audience
- support judgments through reference to the text, other works, other authors, or to personal knowledge (California Department of Education 1997, 52)

Response to Literature Rubric

Borrowing language from the California standards as well as from other published rubrics, Santa Monica High School teachers wrote, adopted, and now continue to revise the five-point rubric for response to literature on page 17.

Every year we find it necessary to revisit the rubric with a fresh set of student essays, taking a professional day to score papers holistically and talk about the instructional implications of what we are finding. The time is well spent because it keeps us "tuned up" in terms of the rubric and helps us be more consistent in our grading. Often we turn to a teacher whose students have fared particularly well and ask what that teacher did to make a difference. Sometimes this gives a normally reticent teacher the opportunity to speak up in a department of twenty-nine talkative English teachers and share a strategy for helping students correct a particularly annoying mechanical error or develop analysis. Teachers new to the department are effusive in their praise for these rubric sessions since it helps build their confidence in grading student essays. They inevitably walk away from the day with ideas for improving instruction.

Response to Literature Rubric
Period _____ Name _____ Score _____

5	5 IDEAS AND EXPLANATIONS (at least three) are insightful, thorough, convincing, varied in strategy, and strongly supported by compelling evidence. 5 ORGANIZATION uses appropriate transitions between and within paragraphs for consistently clear, smooth, and logical relationships among ideas. 5 STYLE is a "pleasure to read"—graceful, uncluttered, rich, and vivid. 5 GRAMMAR AND MECHANICS errors are rare or absent.
4	4 IDEAS AND EXPLANATIONS (at least two) are reasonable, substantial, and supported by well-chosen evidence. 4 ORGANIZATION is logical and appropriate for content, but not as smooth as a 5. 4 STYLE is clear, shows sentence variety, and uses interesting and precise vocabulary. 4 GRAMMAR AND MECHANICS errors are occasional.
3	3 IDEAS AND EXPLANATIONS are mostly on topic and understandable but evidence may be limited and explanations are often too simple, obvious, brief, vague, or illogical. May contain some plot summary or evidence-to-inference. 3 ORGANIZATION maintains one idea per paragraph, but is simplistic *or* idea relationships are sometimes unclear. 3 STYLE is functional but sentence variety and vocabulary are limited *or* style is lively but wordy. 3 GRAMMAR AND MECHANICS errors are frequent.
2	2 IDEAS AND EXPLANATIONS are too simple, very repetitious, hard to follow, mostly irrelevant, inaccurate, and/or contain mostly plot summary. 2 ORGANIZATION shows some minor skill but has major flaws—e.g., no controlling idea; poor paragraphing; redundant sections. 2 STYLE has major flaws—e.g., simplistic, wordy, repetitious, monotonous, often unclear. 2 GRAMMAR AND MECHANICS errors exist in almost every sentence and may interfere with meaning.
1	1 IDEAS AND EXPLANATIONS are absent, irrelevant, unsupported by evidence, or incomprehensible. 1 ORGANIZATION lacks paragraphing and is illogical and confusing *or* essay is too short to have any organization. 1 STYLE has such severe flaws that sentences are hard to understand *or* essay is too short to judge. 1 GRAMMAR AND MECHANICS errors are pervasive and obstruct meaning *or* essay is too short to judge grammar/mechanics.

In an ideal world—one that I have yet to inhabit—an English department would post anchor papers for each rubric score on their website. We are working to make this happen, but there never seems to be time enough. Scored essays with teacher commentary offer parents tangible evidence of the kind of writing teachers try to foster. The revelatory act of going public with anchor papers helps lift the veil of mystery that often surrounds writing. One way to ease the burden from teachers' shoulders is to share the load. The more others understand what we are looking for in student papers, the more likely students are to give us what we want.

This sample paper was written by an eleventh grader to a prompt that asked students to read an excerpt from Richard Rodriguez's *Hunger of Memory*, describing a family Christmas. Students were asked to analyze the narrator's relationship with his family using specific evidence from the passage to support their thesis. The paper was scored as a 3.

The Prompt

In the passage written by Richard Rodriguez he describes a Christmas where his family is gathered up. Richard's mother had a dream that her children would become rich and buy her a lot of presents for Christmas when she became old. As Rodriguez describes this particular Christmas he tells us how his mother's dream came true.

Student Essay

Richard seems to really care about his family, he really cares about his parents. "I am tempted to ask her quickly if there is anything wrong." Its you can see this shows how he worries about what's going on with his mother. He seems to be very close to her.

"I take it to my father and place it on him. In that instant I feel the thinness of his arms. He turns . . . I realize, the only thing that he has said to me all evening." I think that Richard and his father are scared to let each other know her they feel. They didn't say anything to each other the whole night, especially being Christmas so I figured that they don't really talk much.

Somehow, even though everybody cares for each other it seems that during Christmas they just spent it together as if it were a responsibility because everybody seems kind of bored just waiting for an opportunity to leave. "children are falling asleep. Someone gets up to leave prompting others to leave." This is one of the reasons why I think that they are being sort of forced to be at the family Christmas party.

In conclusion I can't really describe his relationship with his family because I would have to know more about his sisters and his brothers.

—Liliana Morales

Teacher Commentary

This paper was assigned a 3 on the rubric. Although the student has a thesis, it is a misreading of the passage. As the writer develops her evidence, instead of supporting her main idea, it contradicts the point she set out to make about the mother's dream coming true. The few examples that are offered are inappropriate to her argument. The writer is not drawing accurate inferences from her evidence. The essay also contains mechanical errors common to first-draft, timed writing.

Many state departments of education are working to provide sample student papers with teacher commentary on their websites. As accountability for performance on writing assessments increases, such transparency is essential. Parents need to know why their child's paper didn't measure up.

Advanced Placement rubrics offer greater discrimination by employing a nine-point scale. I like having more levels to work with, and they allow students to see gradations of improvement over time. The following is a generic rubric that works well for analytical essays about literature. To give you some idea of how I translate these numbers into grades: 9 = A+, 8 = A, 7 = A–, 6 = B+, 5 = B, 4 = B–, 3 = C, 2 = D, 1 = F.

A Nine-Point Rubric for Writing About Literature

An 8–9 essay responds to the prompt clearly, directly, and fully. This paper approaches the text analytically, supports a coherent thesis with evidence from the text, and explains how the evidence illustrates and reinforces its thesis. The essay employs subtlety in its use of the text; the writer's style is fluent and flexible. It is also free of mechanical and grammatical errors.

A 6–7 essay responds to the assignment clearly and directly but with less development than an 8–9 paper. It demonstrates a good understanding of the text and supports its thesis with appropriate textual evidence. While its approach is analytical, the analysis is less precise than in the 8 or 9 essay, and its use of the text is competent but not subtle. The writing in this paper is forceful and clear with few if any grammatical and mechanical errors.

A 5 essay addresses the assigned topic intelligently but does not answer it fully and specifically. It is characterized by a good but general grasp of the text using the text to frame an apt response to the prompt. It may employ textual evidence sparingly or offer evidence without attaching it to the thesis. The essay is clear and organized but may be somewhat mechanical. The paper may also be marred by grammatical and mechanical errors.

A 3–4 essay fails in some important way to fulfill the demands of the prompt. It may not address part of the assignment; it may fail to provide adequate textual support for its thesis or base its analysis on a misreading of some part of the text. This essay may present one or more incisive insights among others of less value. The writing may be similarly uneven in development with lapses in organization, clarity, grammar, and mechanics.

A 1–2 essay commonly combines two or more serious failures. It may not address the actual assignment; it may indicate a serious misreading of the text; it may not offer textual evidence or may use it in a way that suggests a failure to understand the text; it may be unclear, badly written, or unacceptably brief. The style of this paper is usually marked by egregious errors. Occasionally a paper in this range is smoothly written but devoid of content.

Persuasive Writing Rubric

During the past school year, teachers in my department realized that we needed to refine our rubric a bit for persuasive essays. Most of our writing assignments in English classes had traditionally focused on literature, but the California standards—like most standards in the nation—also require students to master persuasive writing. Students are expected to be able to:

- structure ideas and arguments in a sustained and logical fashion
- use specific rhetorical devices to support assertions (e.g., appeal to logic through reasoning; appeal to emotion or ethical belief; relate a personal anecdote, case study, or analogy)
- clarify and defend positions with precise and relevant evidence, including facts, expert opinions, quotations, and expressions of commonly accepted beliefs and logical reasoning
- address readers' concerns, counterclaims, biases, and expectations

The rubric on page 22 employs the same framework as our response-to-literature scoring guide with the addition of features essential for effective persuasive writing.

This rubric provides teachers with a tool for handling the paper load. Ideally I would execute the process described in Chapter 1 for every essay my students write. Unfortunately, this is not possible. If my students are writing a five- to- seven-hundred-word essay—the guidelines recommended in the California standards—every three to four weeks, I must occasionally abandon paragon pedagogy and re-sort to holistic assessment. I justify this practice in the knowledge that students learn from the practice of writing as well as from my considered responses. When I teach two periods of the same course I will often split the difference by correcting and commenting on the essays of one class and scoring the second set with the rubric. For the next essay the other class receives detailed feedback. It is not an ideal system but it keeps students writing and keeps me from throwing in the towel.

On the rubric I highlight the phrases that describe student performance. In many cases students' essays exhibit features from several of the categories. For example, while a paper might be a 4 in terms of organization, its lack of clarity and the proliferation of mechanical errors might earn it a 3. The highlighted scoring guide

PERSUASIVE WRITING RUBRIC

5	5 IDEAS AND EXPLANATIONS (at least two) are insightful, thorough, convincing, and supported by a variety of compelling evidence that appeals to both logic and emotion. Explains the main opposing arguments and offers strong rebuttal. 5 ORGANIZATION uses appropriate transitions between and within paragraphs for consistently clear, smooth, and logical relationships among ideas. 5 STYLE is a "pleasure to read"—graceful, uncluttered, rich, and vivid. 5 GRAMMAR AND MECHANICS errors are rare or absent.
4	4 IDEAS AND EXPLANATIONS (at least two) are reasonable, substantial, and supported by relevant evidence that appeals to both logic and emotion. Explains opposing arguments and offers rebuttal. 4 ORGANIZATION is logical and appropriate for content, but not as smooth as a 5. 4 STYLE is clear, shows sentence variety, and uses interesting and precise vocabulary. 4 GRAMMAR AND MECHANICS errors are occasional.
3	3 IDEAS AND EXPLANATIONS are mostly understandable and on topic, but evidence is limited and explanations are often too simple, obvious, brief, vague, or illogical. May mention opposing arguments, but rebuttal is weak or absent; may ignore key opposing arguments. 3 ORGANIZATION maintains one idea per paragraph, but is simplistic *or* idea relationships are sometimes unclear. 3 STYLE is functional but sentence variety and vocabulary are limited *or* style is lively but wordy. 3 GRAMMAR AND MECHANICS errors are frequent.
2	2 IDEAS AND EXPLANATIONS are too simple, brief, vague, repetitious, hard to follow, irrelevant, weakly supported, and/or inaccurate. 2 ORGANIZATION shows some minor skill but has major flaws—e.g., no controlling idea; poor paragraphing; redundant sections. 2 STYLE has major flaws—e.g., simplistic, wordy, repetitious, monotonous, often unclear. 2 GRAMMAR AND MECHANICS errors exist in almost every sentence and may interfere with meaning.
1	1 IDEAS AND EXPLANATIONS are absent, irrelevant, unsupported by evidence, or incomprehensible. 1 ORGANIZATION lacks paragraphing and is illogical and confusing *or* essay is too short to have any organization. 1 STYLE has such severe flaws that sentences are hard to understand *or* essay is too short to judge. 1 GRAMMAR AND MECHANICS errors are pervasive and obstruct meaning *or* essay is too short to judge grammar/mechanics.

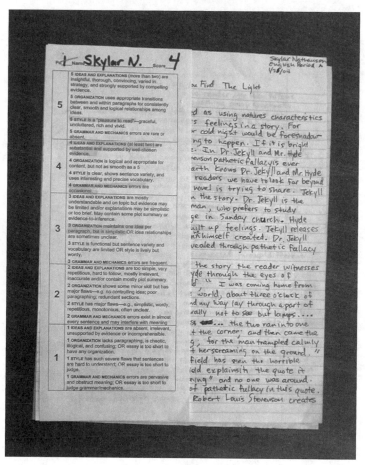

FIGURE 2–1 *Student Essay with Highlighted Rubric Attached*

provides students with a bit more information than a bald numeric score and allows me to further refine the process by assigning papers scores like 4/3 or 4–. As this is a classroom assignment, not a high-stakes assessment, the fuzzy numbers work. When returning papers I take time to review the rubric, talk about common errors that I saw in the papers, and post sample papers that got the job done. Rather

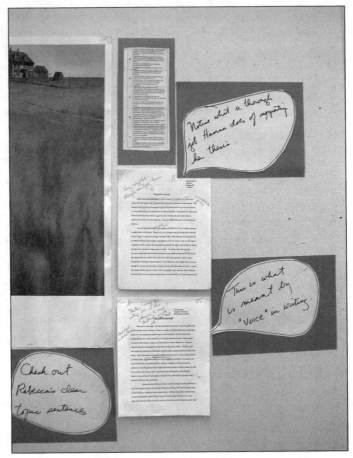

FIGURE 2–2 *Classroom Bulletin Board with Posted Essays*

than simply displaying the best essays from the usual suspects, I point out in comic-strip-like balloons what particular writers did well:

Notice what a compelling first sentence Laeticia wrote.

Check out how these supporting paragraphs are linked with effective transitions.

Don't you wish you had come up with a terrific title like Sam's?

Look at how this "expert opinion" strengthened Marcie's argument.

To help students make sense of my limited feedback and internalize assessment guidelines, I ask them to write notes to themselves offering advice for their next essay. I encourage students to borrow language from the rubric and from the standards.

Dear Max,
You forgot to address the reader's concerns and biases. Also remember not to use quotation marks when you indent and single space long quotations. Also your conclusions are usually lame. Don't start the paragraph with "Finally"!

Your friend,
Max

Dear Azadeh,
The organization of this persuasive essay wasn't very logical. I think it would have been better to save your best idea for last. And why do you always forget to include a title? It's not that hard. Next time don't start so many sentences with "He." It makes the essay sound babyish.

Sincerely,
Azadeh

Dear Grace,
In your next essay, think about using a personal anecdote for evidence. You are good at telling stories. Also try to avoid clichés. It will help make your essay more persuasive not to settle for tired old sayings. You also tend to repeat yourself rather than exploring your ideas.

Love always,
Grace

Dear Brian,
Try to proofread more carefully next time. Turn on spell-check. You also know more words than you are using. Remember what Mrs. Jago said about more concrete nouns and stronger verbs.

Brian

I collect these notes and hand them back while students are rewriting their next essay. It seems to me that writing advice to themselves in their own hand holds real potential for long-term learning.

Informative Writing Scoring Guide

Our Santa Monica High School rubrics are not perfect. Their greatest value has consisted in the collaborative process we used to construct them. Another model you might consider for developing your own rubrics is the National Assessment of Educational Progress (NAEP) writing scoring guide. NAEP employs descriptors rather than numbers though one could easily adapt it to a six-point or A–F format. The rubric on pages 27–28 was designed to assess twelfth-grade informative writing. According to NAEP:

> Informative writing focuses primarily on the subject-matter element in communication. This type of writing is used to share knowledge and to convey messages, instructions, and ideas. Like all writing, informative writing may be filtered through the writer's impressions, understanding, and feelings. Used as a means of exploration, informative writing helps both the writer and the reader to learn new ideas and to reexamine old conclusions. Informative writing may also involve reporting on events or experiences, or analyzing concepts and relationships, including developing hypotheses and generalizations. Any of these types of informative writing can be based on the writer's personal knowledge and experience or on information newly presented to the writer that must be understood in order to complete a task. Usually, informative writing involves a mix of the familiar and the new, and both are clarified in the process of writing. Depending on the task, writing based on either personal experience or factual information may span the range of thinking skills from recall to analysis to evaluation.

The NAEP website, http://nces.ed.gov/nationsreportcard/writing/
,
is a treasure trove of useful material for writing teachers, including released writing prompts, sample student essays, and results from the 2002 assessment. Along with grading papers, writing teachers often carry the additional burden of creating a writing curriculum out of whole cloth. Designing prompts and finding sample student papers is labor intensive. Why not use models that have been vetted by

NAEP INFORMATIVE WRITING RUBRIC

Excellent
- Information is presented effectively and consistently supported with well-chosen details.
- Information is focused and well organized, with a sustained controlling idea and effective use of transitions.
- Response consistently exhibits variety in sentence structure and precision in word choice.
- Errors in grammar, spelling, and punctuation are few and do not interfere with understanding.

Skillful
- Information is presented clearly and supported with pertinent details in much of the response.
- Response is well organized, but may lack some transitions.
- Response exhibits some variety in sentence structure and uses good word choice; occasionally, words may be used inaccurately.
- Errors in grammar, spelling, and punctuation do not interfere with understanding.

Sufficient
- Information is presented clearly and supported with some pertinent details.
- Information is generally organized, but has few or no transitions among parts.
- Sentence structure may be simple and unvaried; word choice is mostly accurate.
- Errors in grammar, spelling, and punctuation do not interfere with understanding.

Uneven
May be characterized by one or more of the following:

- Information is presented clearly in parts; other parts are undeveloped or repetitive *or* is no more than a well-written beginning.
- Organized in parts of the response; other parts are disjointed and/or lack transitions.
- Exhibits uneven control over sentence boundaries and sentence structure; may exhibit some inaccurate word choices.
- Errors in grammar, spelling, and punctuation sometimes interfere with understanding.

continued

NAEP INFORMATIVE WRITING RUBRIC (*continued*)

Insufficient

May be characterized by one or more of the following:

- Provides information that is very undeveloped or list-like.
- Much of the response is disorganized or unfocused, *or* the response is too brief to detect organization.
- Author has minimal control over sentence boundaries and sentence structure; word choice may often be inaccurate.
- Errors in grammar, spelling, and punctuation interfere with understanding in much of the response.

Unsatisfactory

May be characterized by one or more of the following:

- Responds to prompt but may be incoherent *or* provides very minimal information *or* merely paraphrases the prompt.
- Little or no apparent organization.
- Minimal or no control over sentence boundaries and sentence structure; word choice may be inaccurate in much or all of the response.
- Errors in grammar, spelling, and punctuation severely impede understanding across the response.

professionals in the field? Before my tenth-grade students wrote to the NAEP informative prompt below, we looked at the student essays posted on the NAEP website that were designated as excellent and skillful. We discussed how these papers met the demands outlined in the scoring guide. It helped students start to see what they were aiming for.

NAEP Informative Writing Prompt

A novel written in the 1950s describes a world where people are not allowed to read books. A small group of people who want to save books memorize them, so that the books won't be forgotten. For example, an old man who has memorized the novel *The Call of the Wild* helps a young boy memorize it by reciting the story to him. In this way, the book is saved for the future.

If you were told that you could save just one book for future generations, which book would you choose?

Write an essay in which you discuss which book you would choose to save for future generations and what it is about the book that makes it important to save. Be sure to discuss in detail why the book is important to you and why it would be important to future generations.

It is unclear to me why NAEP didn't identify *Fahrenheit 451* in the prompt. I told students that Ray Bradbury's novel was the book being referred to. One of the things that attracted me to the prompt was that many of my students had read *Fahrenheit 451* as ninth graders. Students cheered when they read the prompt, thinking that it would be enjoyable to write to. I pay attention to such unsought feedback. A prompt that appeals to students is often one they perform well on. Rather than trying to impress you with the successful essays, I offer a student draft that clearly falls in the "Uneven" to "Insufficient" range.

The Catcher in the Rye

If, just like in the novel *Fahrenheit 451*, books were being burned and only a few books could of been saved one of those books should definitely be the great novel *A Catcher in the Rye* by J. D. Salinger. It is a classic book that everyone can relate to. The loss of this book would mean the loss of a really important part of our culture. This book would be a treasure for future generations. No matter how young or old the reader is they can always relate to this book.

This book is very symbolic of many very human things. For example, in this book J. D. Salinger tells about a part of the story were the main character, Holden Caulfield, goes to the museum he went to as a child this is one of the few places he enjoys and one of the few places that is not phoney to him because its always the same. This time shows how Holden dislikes change. Everyone can relate to a time in their life where they wish something wouldn't change. It can teach many people many important lessons about life.
—Honey S.
Period 1

Honey struggles with developing her ideas fully. Knowing this, I invited her to an individual conference. While the rest of the class was engaged in peer editing, I asked her to read her draft aloud and talk to me about which of the NAEP scoring guide categories best described what she had written.

Honey: Well, I guess somebody would say this is just a beginning, but honest, Mrs. Jago, I couldn't think of anything else to write.

Mrs. J: Let's look at places where you left me wanting more. One sentence that leaps out at me is where you mention the museum. I'm not sure I understand how the museum not changing—this is a terrific insight—means it isn't phony.

Honey: You know how Holden is always calling everybody a phony all over the place in the book.

Mrs. J: Yes, but you are talking about the museum here. Maybe you could add another paragraph about what Holden sees as phony in everyone around him.

Honey: You mean like his roommate?

Mrs. J: Whomever you think.

Honey: Hmm . . . I guess. Or how Phoebe isn't phony.

Mrs. J: Good idea. Why don't you jot down that point while you're thinking of it. (*Honey writes*)

Mrs. J: Is there anything else you could say about the museum? What was it about the place or in the place that Holden liked so much?

Honey: You think I should put in a quote there?

Mrs. J: It's up to you. That would help to provide those "pertinent details" we talked about that skillful essays include.

Honey: It would make the thing longer, too.

Mrs. J: Right. It would. Do you want to make a note of that? (*Honey writes*)

Mrs. J: Your last sentence talks about the novel teaching people important lessons. What lessons did you learn from reading *The Catcher in the Rye?*

Honey: I have to think about that.

Mrs. J: OK. Give it some thought, and we'll talk more. Can you come back at lunch?

Honey: Today?

Mrs. J: Well, we might as well work on this now while the book is still fresh in your mind, don't you think?

Honey: Yeah. OK.

Would all students have benefited from such one-on-one attention? Of course they would, but there simply isn't enough of me to go around. Triage is the best I can offer. In this case the four students in the class of thirty-six who most needed help received it.

THREE

Leave It to Machines!

Imagine a world where students write their essays on laptop computers light enough to be carried around in their backpacks and as inexpensive as a cellular phone. In some programs students have only to hit "Send" for the paper to arrive at your computer where you type "grade" and a software program reads and assesses the students' work. Within seconds you receive a report for the entire class. You press a few more keys and receive a breakdown of how students performed in terms of content, organization, style, and mechanics. With other programs students click "Get My Score" and have their paper evaluated without ever going through a teacher. Am I dreaming or is such a world within the horizon of possibility? According to researchers in the field, this and more will soon be at your fingertips. Computer scoring is a thing of the present, not the future. This brave new world is already our world.

A Brief History of Computer Scoring

In 1966 Ellis Page and colleagues introduced the Project Essay Grade (PEG) program, which assessed student writing primarily on the superficial features of the text: document length, word rarity, and punctuation. His underlying theory is that there are intrinsic qualities to a person's writing style measurable by computer that correspond to human graders' assessments. Research on PEG over thirty years consistently reports high correlations between PEG and human graders (Page, Poggio, and Keith 1997). For more information, go to http://134.68.49.185 /pegdemo/ref.asp.

Other computer scoring processes judge the thoroughness of an essay's content by examining the information it contains. Recent research has trained computers to recognize aspects of creative writing and, as a result, to deliver scores for narrative as well as content-based prompts. A software program is fed information about a topic—from fifty thousand to ten million words—and assigns a mathematical degree of similarity or difference between the meaning of each word and any other word. This allows students to use synonyms without being penalized. The computer is also fed sample papers graded by a human scorer who may or may not be the students' teacher. The computer takes the combination of words in each student essay and calculates its similarity to the combination of words in the comparison essays. The student receives the same grade as the human-graded essays to which it is most closely matched. Researchers insist that there is a strong correlation between students who write the most and those who write the best. Those who know a lot write a lot. Hence, length is often a factor in scoring. Longer papers tend to score higher.

Educational Testing Service's Electronic Essay Rater (e-rater) uses a combination of these processes as well as measures syntactic variety, counting the number of complement, subordinate, infinitive, and relative clauses as well as occurrences of modal verbs (would, could) to determine an essay's score. Researchers took essays that had been graded by teachers and looked for signs the computer could use to predict those human judgments. The goal of the program is to judge the structure and coherence of the writing rather than the quality of the thoughts or originality of the prose.

E-rater results have been so impressive that it is now used to score the General Management Aptitude Test (GMAT) and is being considered for use in the Graduate Record Examination. Testing experts predict that computers will eventually be grading essays for SAT and ACT college admissions tests. The GMAT website states, "e-rater and independent readers agree, on average, 87 percent to 94 percent of the time." For more information, go to www.ets.org/research /erater.html.

Classroom Tools for Online Scoring

Educational Testing Service's Criterion Online Writing Evaluation Program is a classroom-based tool offering students writing practice and feedback to which their teachers might not otherwise provide access. Students write to a prompt and are evaluated within seconds on everything from grammar and spelling to style and organization. Essays are returned to students with highlighted portions flagging particular errors. If students click on these lines, they receive further diagnostic suggestions for improvement. Teachers can choose from a bank of 108 writing prompts spanning all grade levels and writing types: narrative, expository, and persuasive.

Textbook publishers offer similar online essay scoring programs. The scoring system I know best is the one offered by Holt, Rinehart and Winston, Holt Online Essay Scoring, because this is the language arts textbook series my district adopted. Their online scoring program provides teachers with prompts to which students write. Dialogue boxes in the software offer students suggestions for

- prewriting and writing tips
- revision tips
- interactive graphic organizers

The publisher's suggestions for helping students begin to write are fully consistent with what is professionally accepted as coherent writing instruction. Students write inside an on-screen box. When the student has finished writing, the computer responds with a holistic score and detailed feedback derived from the scoring rubric. Holistic scores are either on a four- or six-point scale, according to the student's state of residence. A ninth-grade student submitted his draft of a persuasive essay and received a computer response:

Writing Prompt

Your principal is considering a new grading policy that replaces letter or number grades on report cards with pass or fail. What is your position concerning this issue? Write a letter to your principal stating your position and supporting it with convincing reasons. Be sure to explain your reasons in detail.

Student Essay

Dear Dr. Straus,

I believe grades are better than pass or fail marks. The reason is because kids won't work hard for a plain P. Grades are what we are used to and what our parents expect.

For example, in history class I would loaf if all I had to do was work for a P instead of for a grade. My parents expect me to get good grades and will be mad at me if I don't. When I see my grade moving down towards a C, I get energized. It is hard to get F's. You have to do no work at all.

Please do not change your policy.

Sincerely,
Marcus

Computer Response

On a four-point scale, here's your score: 1

1 This response demonstrates emerging effort with persuasive writing. For the most part, the essay:
- shows little awareness for the topic and purpose for writing
- lacks organization
- offers unclear and confusing ideas
- shows minimal persuasive reasoning or elaboration
- exhibits major problems with control of written language

The student can then click a link to receive

- analytic feedback on five dimensions of his or her writing: content and development, focus and organization, effective sentences, word choice and grammar, usage and mechanics.
- writing activities to improve his writing, geared to the holistic score point.
- an interactive model student essay on the same prompt. By rolling over the model, the student highlights aspects of the model that explain why it is effective.

Here is what Marcus was "told" about his writing:

Content and Development: Your essay shows *emerging* ability for this trait. For the most part, the essay:

- uses superficial, unclear, or confusing ideas
- lacks elaboration and support

Focus and Organization: Your essay shows *emerging* ability for this trait. For the most part, the essay:

- shows little attempt to address the prompt
- shows no awareness of audience
- displays little, if any, organization
- lacks unity and completeness

Effective Sentences: Your essays shows *limited* ability for this trait. For the most part, the essay:

- exhibits limited sentence correctness; may contain several major errors
- demonstrates limited sentence quality; may contain several awkward sentences
- displays limited variety in sentence types, lengths, structures, and beginnings
- displays limited fluency

Word Choice: Your essays shows *emerging* ability for this trait. For the most part, the essay:

- uses words that may not be appropriate to audience and purpose
- uses vague or inaccurate words that may interfere with clarity and meaning

Grammar, Usage, and Mechanics: Your essay shows *competent* ability for this trait. For the most part, the essay:

- demonstrates general command of language conventions
- exhibits general command of spelling, punctuation, and capitalization

The computer's responses are taken from the scoring rubric and as such employ the academic language of writing instruction. Students will need to be familiar with this language in order to make sense of their feedback. You will notice that Marcus' persuasive essay was deemed competent in grammar, usage, and mechanics yet still received the lowest score of 1. When I saw these results, I asked Marcus to tell me what he thought he might do, based on this computer feedback, to improve his letter.

Marcus: Well, I guess write more. I don't think the computer likes short essays.

Mrs. J: Why do you say that?

Marcus: I'd hit send and it would send me a message that said, "not enough." (*The message actually reads: Your essay is too short to score.*

FIGURE 3–1 *Computer Scoring, Marcus*

Please develop it further and then try again.) I would add a sentence and hit Send again and I'd get the same message back. I'd add another sentence, same thing. Finally, it stopped.

Mrs. J: We've talked before about how your essays lack development, haven't we?

Marcus: Yeah, so maybe you told the computer to say this to me.

Mrs. J: Maybe the computer and I just agree.

Marcus: Well, I like short. You don't make so many mistakes with short essays. See how I did OK on the grammar?

Mrs. J: That was good. What do you think you might have added if you did want to make the letter longer?

Marcus: I dunno.

Mrs. J: Do you remember how we talked about persuasive writing, that it needed to address the concerns of the audience? Can you think of any reasons why Mrs. Straus might want to go to a pass/fail system?

Marcus: Not really. It's stupid.

Mrs. J: But what if students who would pass with a D under the old system now got Fs and no credit for the course? Don't you think some students would work harder for a P?

Marcus: I suppose a principal might think that's a good idea. Yeah, that would be good to add. I don't have to write this again, do I?

Mrs. J: No, but why don't you take a look at the student essay that earned a 4.

Along with feedback based on a score, students are also offered links to writing activities to improve their writing and a model student essay for this particular prompt. I don't pretend for a minute that this experience of online writing and scoring transformed Marcus as a writer. It did, however, forcefully support the substance of my comments about his essays.

The development process for online tools such as ETS's Criterion and Holt, Rinehart and Winston's Online Essay Scoring begins with the crafting of prompts and creation of a rubric. Sample student essays are then collected and scored by trained readers. These scores and the student essays are entered into the computer. The program uses the papers scored by human readers to create a scoring model against which future student writing is compared. While not infallible, machine scoring is reliable. Subtle or ironic essays can be misread.

Human readers are not infallible, either. I remember an essay I received last year from Fionnan O'Connor, an absolutely brilliant tenth grader who wrote his paper on *The Catcher in the Rye* entirely in the voice of Holden. I am not usually so dense as to miss something like this but marked the paper in lots of red and with a large C and an "Inappropriate" at the top. When Fionnan rather sheepishly asked me to reread his essay, I agreed but wondered why. Finally the penny dropped. I know I grade inconsistently when tired or cranky after seeing repeated errors I know I have taught exhaustively. Online scoring tools are perfectly consistent. Unlike me, my computer is never bored, rushed, sleepy, impatient, or forgetful. It is not influenced by what a student's last paper looked like and how much improvement might have been made. I would never turn the grading of student essays over to a computer any more than I would turn it over to an outside reader. Reading their writing is how I get to know my students and see their minds at work. I just need support. Computer scoring is another tool that I use to lighten the load from time to time.

Educators' Concerns

David Bloome, a past president of the National Council of Teachers of English and professor of education at Vanderbilt University, worries that the context and audience for student writing may become as artificial as the medium and that students will learn to write for computers rather than for real people. "One of the things that we hope that students will learn as they learn about writing is how to use all of the resources that are involved in our language system to express meanings, to be creative, to express emotion, to be persuasive. While this may include the so-called foundations, we need to be careful that any of those tools we use as teachers do not work against our pedagogical goals." Bloome is concerned that such electronic aids will be seen by some as "making unnecessary the professional knowledge that teachers need to effectively respond to student writing" (Manzo 2003).

In an *English Journal* essay Julie Cheville, professor of language and linguistics at Rutgers University and director of a National Writing Project site, warns:

> Automated scoring technologies require our vigilance. Criterion and other error-driven programs like it are increasingly available to individual districts and schools. They are promoted in a host of ways: as instructional complements to writing-process instruction, as vehicles to consistent writing and evaluation across the curriculum, and as professional development tools. How, then, can teachers, teacher educators, and professional organizations resist such a sales pitch? What do we know about language that makes clear what automated technologies simply cannot do? (2004, 49)

Automated grading programs work best for content-based essays where the prompt asks students to demonstrate what they know about a subject citing evidence that has been taught. Responses to literature that depend on personal and original insight into a text are more problematic, though responses to literature have been computer-scored effectively. It all depends on the training sets the computer is trained with. Often educators oppose computerized assessment of writing doubting that any machine can judge an argument's cogency or grasp linguistic nuances the way a live teacher can. We know that a computer can't replace a teacher— nor should it. What online scoring provides is more opportunities for students to write and receive feedback, on prompts similar to those they encounter on state assessments.

A further criticism of electronic scoring of student papers has come from those who lament the loss of collegiality that proliferated at large-scale scoring sessions. These events brought large numbers of teachers together, fed them thousands of student papers, and built consensus around what teachers mean by "good writing." The scoring sessions fostered collegiality and encouraged conversations about pedagogy and practice. They also gave teachers a sense of ownership of the process. These powerful professional development moments will not be easy or inexpensive to reproduce.

My greatest concern has to do with access. I am extremely fortunate to have ten up-to-date, working Macintosh computers in my classroom. This is only the case because I am the school yearbook advisor. Most English classrooms have one or two computers at most. Yes, they are all wired to the Internet, but this is a far cry from meeting the needs of all students. Almost all schools have computer labs, but it requires careful planning to schedule one's class for the day, and one can never monopolize the facilities for more than two days in a row. It makes sense that software companies are ahead of the curve, but we need to be careful not to promote practices that are simply not possible for most teachers to implement. Whenever I assign a timed writing, the first ten students who come to class and wish to write on a computer may use the machines. It's not fair, but it's the best I can do.

My Reader Is a Computer

While electronic assessment of student writing is arguably in the best interests of companies and of states that need to score large numbers of papers as inexpensively as possible, I think it also offers hope to overworked teachers. Online grading programs provide teachers with another way for students to write more while the teacher reads less.

Twenty years ago my school used their Gifted and Talented Education (GATE) program funding to provide teachers of honors classes with readers. At the time our students were identified as Mentally Gifted Minors. This assistance was a godsend, allowing me to assign more essays without sacrificing sleep. I had the trained reader score student papers for grammar, mechanics, organization, and supporting evidence and then quickly read them myself for content. The system worked beautifully. Subsequent budget constraints and new GATE funding guidelines have, sadly, forced us to discontinue the practice. As a result, teachers assigned fewer papers. Online scoring provides me with an electronic reader and offers my students additional opportunities for practice. Availing ourselves of electronic resources is not a sin. It's a strategy for survival.

FOUR

Misery Loves Company

From: "thais" thais@mail.smmusd.org
To: Santa Monica High School English Department
Date: Wed, 18 Feb. 2004 20:53:22 -0800

Colleagues—

Our first Grading Party is this Saturday morning, February 21, in the Santa Monica High School Library! The schedule is below.

If you don't plan to come for the earliest session, please time your arrival so you enter during the 9:15–9:30 AM break.

The PTSA is funding bagels, juice, and Starbucks coffee, all of which will be available at the library. If you need a rather steady coffee flow, bring your first cup with you and then refill from our supply.

SCHEDULE—All times are SHARP, so if you want to chat and eat a bit before Session 1, please arrive before 7:45.
7:30–8:00 Coffee, juice, bagels, socializing, staking out your spot
8:00–9:15 Session 1
9:15–9:30 Break
9:30–10:45 Session 2
10:45–11:00 Break
11:00–12:00 Session 3

RULES:
—No noise or other distractions during grading sessions.
—Eating is OK, but quiet food only, please.
—Enter and depart at break times.
And always remember the Grading Party motto: Misery LOVES company.

Rob Thais and Cathy Marsh

The idea for organizing grading parties grew out of conversations between Rob Thais and Cathy Flores Marsh regarding the difficulty they were having disciplining themselves to grade papers. Cathy, a new teacher, was relieved to hear that a veteran like Rob suffered the same pangs of guilt as she about the pile of papers on their desks. She was also worried that not returning student papers in a timely manner distorted her curriculum. She felt she couldn't move forward into a new unit until she had completed the last and resorted to classroom activities that filled up the days until she could catch up with the papers. It bothered her that these lessons weren't as rigorous and focused as she would like. Rob confessed that he had been known to take a personal day and stay home just to catch up with his student papers.

Figuring that other members of the department likely shared the same problem and the same guilt, they approached our school librarian about opening the school library on Saturdays, and the PTSA president about providing refreshments for an English department gathering where teachers would come together with their stacks of unread papers to lend moral support to one another. Instead of feeling as if they were giving up their weekend to schoolwork, teachers could feel professional about their work and less alone in their struggle. Most teachers in the department meet between 140 and 180 students a day. Our department standards—determined by us—require that students write one process paper during every six-week grading period. The load was demoralizing us, taking its toll on our ability to teach.

FIGURE 4–1 *Grading Party: Gilda and Cathy*

Grading Parties

Surrounding ourselves with colleagues helps us teachers keep grading. We draw strength from our collective willpower. In this regard grading papers is much like exercising. It is so much easier to go out for exercise while walking and talking with a friend than it is to cover those miles alone. Coming together on a Saturday was a way to meet our professional commitment professionally. Cathy explains:

> There were many things I enjoy about our grading parties. The first is that there was a sense of camaraderie. It was a "we're all in this together" kind of feeling. It was comforting to see that I was not the only person who had a mound of potentially horrible essays to grade.

I also liked having access to the opinions of my colleagues. I was able to ask for advice and get immediate responses, causing a dialogue that was *always* beneficial to me. In addition, we were able to talk about each other and our personal lives, something we do not get to truly experience at a school our size. Not only do the kids get lost in the shuffle but, oftentimes, so do we. As a new teacher last year, it felt like I was establishing friends at the school on a different level. And lastly, we were able to gossip, frolic, be sarcastic, and simply vent to our colleagues what our spouses did not understand.

Santa Monica High School has an English department of twenty-nine teachers ranging from lifetime members like myself with over thirty years in the classroom to first-year teachers. Under normal circumstances we have minimal time to work together. Our school has negotiated "buy-back" time with our union, and every Wednesday morning students begin classes at 9:30 AM so that teachers can have approximately two hours of uninterrupted, high-quality professional development time. Each month, two Wednesdays are dedicated to house meetings (our school is divided into six smaller houses); one Wednesday is dedicated to departments, another to faculty meetings or personal professional work. Meeting monthly offers hardly enough time for a department as large as ours to discuss critical issues; it certainly does not allow us to run scoring sessions or discuss student work. Experienced teachers had little time to share what we knew with new teachers. We were hungry for more time together. We needed each other.

The National Commission on Teaching and America's Future report *No Dream Denied, A Pledge to America's Children* states, "Teaching is the only profession in which entry-level individuals are expected—from Day One—to do the same job and perform at the same level of competence as experienced practitioners. Our schools regularly put rookies in the starting lineup and are surprised when they strike out" (2003, 27). We are fortunate at Santa Monica High School to be able to attract highly qualified young teachers to our site, but we don't always take care of them very well. In some instances having "stars" in the department intimidates new teachers.

They worry that they are not offering students the caliber of instruction parents expect and that they might have received from an experienced teacher the year before. I worry that that we will lose these bright young things.

No Dream Denied identifies peer review and assistance as one of the features of a successful professional learning community.

> Mentoring for new teachers is the first step on a path that leads to the career-long community of support needed to undergird accomplished teaching. Peer assistance and peer review support further career development. Peer assistance aims at helping new and veteran teachers improve their knowledge and skills by linking new teachers—or struggling veteran teachers—with consulting teachers, to provide continuing support by observing, modeling, sharing ideas and skills, and recommending materials for further study. (27)

The English department grading parties provided an informal setting for teachers to coalesce and become a professional learning community. New teachers were stunned to discover that well-informed, experienced teachers' judgments on student papers can be inconsistent and that this isn't a sign of incompetence but a reflection of the complexity of grading student papers. Given the circumstances under which we work—large class size and a writing-intensive curriculum—all of us struggle. There is something about laughing together over a student sentence in a paper on *Romeo and Juliet*, ". . . because if Claudio and don Pedro never found out that they had made a mistake, Hero would have lived to pretend to be dead for the rest of her life," that helps all of us keep going, keep grading. Logic aside, the metaphysical implications are staggering.

Tisha Reichle, in her fifth year at Santa Monica High School, writes that she attended the grading parties because

> The feeling of camaraderie in the air—a sort of shared torture—kept me alert and the silence (no television, telephone, or "I'm hungry" from the kids) enabled me to focus on the task of reading essays. Misery does, indeed, love company. The grading orgies offered the

FIGURE 4–2   *Grading Party: Rob and Pete*

option to tackle my grading right at the start of a weekend, rather than procrastinate until Sunday night. I left feeling a sense of accomplishment, and was then able to enjoy the rest of my weekend without the guilt embedded in a stack of ungraded papers. Additionally, the camaraderie was enticing; to be able to lament our common situations (in terms of grading and planning) was always something to look forward to!

The National Commission on Teaching and America's Future insists "the nation cannot achieve quality teaching for every child unless teachers can be kept in the classroom. The missing ingredient is finding a way for school systems to organize the work of qualified teacher so they can collaborate with their colleagues in developing strong learning communities that will sustain them as they become more accomplished teachers" (17). Grading parties demonstrated to new teachers that all of us in the English department—however "accomplished" we might be—struggle with the time- and brain-consuming calisthenics of grading student papers. The grading "gymnasium" improved the pain-gain ratio. The gatherings strengthened our professional community by providing an informal setting for reflecting on student writing and considering how to improve instruction. Ideally, teachers would be compensated for such Saturday sessions. Such an eventuality we regard, candidly, as unlikely.

Large-Scale Scoring Sessions Versus Remote Readings

In Chapter 3 I lamented the loss of large-scale scoring sessions to remote or computer-assisted scoring of student writing. Where once large groups of teachers gathered to score thousands of papers over several days, now student writing for many state and the new SAT and ACT exams is scanned into computers and sent out electronically to readers at different places all across the nation. Graders working alone at their home computers are "normed" on a scoring rubric and must read and score a set of anchor papers each time they log in. Supervisors electronically read over their shoulders, and readers who deviate from the accepted norm receive a telephone call for a conversation much like the ones a table leader would have with readers at a scoring session. Two readers score each essay independently and if the scores differ by more than a point, the paper is sent to a third reader. Research indicates that this process works as reliably as the large-scale readings at a fraction of the cost.

George Gadda, former chief reader for the Advanced Placement Language exam, director of Writing Programs at UCLA, and consultant to the College Board for the new SAT writing initiative, explained to a reporter for the *New York Times*, "A lot of us mourn the passage of the old face-to-face grading system. And in principle, I'm not a proponent of doing things online, but logistically the old kind of interchange just isn't possible any more. You couldn't get that many papers graded quickly enough" (McGrath 2004, 27). I am persuaded that student essays will be scored accurately. What is likely to be lost in the process is consensus building by classroom teachers around the nature and features of good student writing.

The College Board is doing everything it can to make their process for scoring essays on the new SAT Writing portion of the exam transparent by providing sample essays with the merits and weaknesses described on their website, www.collegeboard.com. The ACT will include a similar writing component. Here is an example from their website, www.actstudent.org/:

ACT Sample Prompt

Prompts used for the ACT Writing Test will:

- describe an issue relevant to high school students
- ask examinees to write about their perspective on the issue

As a starting place, two different perspectives on the issue will be provided. Examinees may choose to support one of these perspectives or to develop a response based on their own perspective.

The Assignment

In some high schools, many teachers and parents have encouraged the school to adopt a dress code that sets guidelines for what students can wear in the school building. Some teachers and parents support a dress code because they think it will improve the learning environment in the school. Other teachers and parents do not support a dress code because they think it restricts the individual student's freedom of expression. In your opinion, should high schools adopt dress codes for students?

In your essay, take a position on this question. You may write about either one of the two points of view given, or you may present a different point of view on this question. Use specific reasons and examples to support your position.

The standard directions in the second paragraph above will be a part of all prompts used on the ACT Writing Test.

I am an unapologetic and unreformed supporter of the addition of writing to the SAT and ACT tests. Rather than practicing arcane strategies for answering analogies correctly, college-bound students will work harder on their writing. Test preparation for these college entrance exams must include tutoring in writing, the very thing teachers are hard-pressed to offer. In addition, college admissions officers will be able to access the SAT or ACT essay written without assistance and compare it to the student's personal statement. Affluent students often receive professional help with these essays, tightening and sharpening the piece until it sparkles. This practice has always bothered me. I help my seniors garner ideas for personal statements and will assist them with proofreading, but the essay is theirs, not mine. Now with a keystroke anyone making college admissions decisions will be able to get a sense of how the applicant writes without outside help.

With Confidence Comes Speed

Uncertainty, perhaps preeminently, impedes progress on a set of papers. Hemming and hawing over whether an essay deserves a C+ or B– takes time. Many new teachers put papers into tentative piles before assigning grades and only assign scores after they have read the entire stack. While this may be a good strategy for accuracy and fairness, it adds precious hours to the reading task. Common scoring sessions help teachers develop confidence as readers and internalize scoring rubrics. They also help teachers learn to read faster.

To re-create the common understandings about student writing that large-scale scoring sessions used to provide, schools and districts should organize local holistic scoring sessions. Teachers need to chew over the actual meaning of phrases in a scoring rubric and talk about the 4-ness versus the 2-ness of anchor papers. Coming to consensus on writing standards is a messy business. It is also essential. To bring such consensus about, schools must invest in professional development. The National Commission on Teaching Writing in America's Schools and Colleges' report *The Neglected "R"* recommends that "States should provide the financial resources necessary for the additional time and personnel required to make writing a centerpiece of the curriculum"

(2003, 8). One institution that continues to invest in large-scale scoring sessions is the University of California.

Every year toward the end of May, two hundred professors and classroom teachers gather at Berkeley for the Subject A reading. The ostensible task is to assess seventeen thousand essays written by students accepted to UC campuses. Results of this assessment determine students' placement in freshman English classes. I always look forward to the long weekend because it provides me with a measuring stick against which to evaluate my own students' writing. I also learn from listening to what writing teachers at the various UC campuses have to say about high school students' weaknesses. While grading five hundred essays in three days might sound like a holiday in hell, these readings have always been a source of pleasure for me. Just as Santa Monica High School's grading parties helped Cathy Marsh feel more connected to the English department, Subject A readings help me feel more connected to the universities for which I am preparing my students. A few years ago when my son James was still in high school, I came home depressed.

It wasn't the quality of the student writing that depressed me but the warning these eighteen-year-olds' essays issued to me as a parent. The text students had been asked to read and respond to was an essay by Ellen Goodman called "The Cordless Tie That Binds People to Work." Goodman describes how cordless phones and other electronic devices have blurred the line between our work life and our home life. I read paper after paper bemoaning the way their mom or dad's cell phone interrupted family meals, ruined family vacations, and, in short, obfuscated their relationship.

To be sure, most students acknowledged that their parents were working hard in order to offer them a better life. But between the lines was a plaintive cry for attention. I began feeling guilty. Ensuring my undivided attention for more than five minutes requires something just short of a thunderbolt. In the way that some women check their nails, I check my email. I always have student papers available to fill any spare second I can find. Like the parents of these soon-to-be college students, I was so busy working and staying in contact with the world that I feared I was in danger of losing touch with those I love most.

Determined to change my ways and eager to spend more valuable time with James, I returned home. The clock was ticking on his high school years, and I wanted to enjoy every minute we had left together. Full of good intentions, I pushed open his bedroom door. Of course, James was on the phone. So I turned on my computer, checked my email, and pulled out my red pen to grade papers.

FIVE

Peer Assessment and Self-Assessment

Peer assessment once seemed like the answer to a writing teacher's prayers. Decrease the hours you spent grading by having students correct each other's errors. Problem solved. Thousands of versions of peer-editing guideline forms made the rounds in professional development workshops and a peer-editing day became a standard feature of the writing process. Unfortunately, like so many aspects of writing instruction, this technique is more complicated than it at first appears. Will Rogers expressed the drawbacks succinctly, "You can't teach what you don't know any more than you can come back from where you ain't been."

In common with many other teachers, I found that peer groups worked adequately and I felt like an accomplished writing teacher in my honors classes while groups of less-scholarly students wasted the time and even added errors to their peers' essays. Refining the peer-editing worksheets wasn't enough. I needed to rethink this aspect of my instructional program. Instead of asking students to correct one another's errors, I began to focus on having students respond to the content and coherence of one another's drafts. Even the most struggling writers were adequately qualified to offer one another feedback as readers.

Before I could ask students to grapple with even these most basic tenets of peer response, I needed to overcome the primary obstacle of making sure every student had a draft. In a non-honors class I would commonly have fewer than half the class ready with a draft on the days

I set aside for peer response. Threats of dire consequences—lower grades, points off, teacher displeasure—elicited no greater response. Taking the high ground with minilectures on how all writers needed a critical friend had little effect. I resorted to trickery. Although the device is impossible to carry off repeatedly in a semester, students will fall for this a few times a year. I schedule a timed writing, ask students to spend a period answering a prompt, collect their papers, and then return them untouched the next day saying, "Class, I thought about it last night and decided to let you rewrite these essays." Rather than groaning, students typically respond with cheers, "Oh, Mrs. Jago, you are so nice! Thank you." I'm not nice; I'm devious. I just succeeded in maneuvering the class into producing drafts for our next day's work.

Pairing Peers for Guided Response

It seems to me that student writers are able to help one another with the following basic questions:

- Does it make sense?
- Can you follow my argument?
- Where did you get lost?
- What do you need to know or want to know that I haven't told you?

Students need help both giving and receiving even such elementary feedback. If I would simply put them in pairs with these guidelines, few would read their partner's paper with much care or offer many useful comments. I'm not denigrating students by saying this. Constructing an obstacle to performance of the task at hand is often a matter of teenage social unease. Who wants to look like a nerd making teacherlike comments on a paper? How many have the stamina to struggle through hard-to-read handwriting? Where does a student find the confidence to suggest improvement in someone else's paper when they know their own writing skills are inadequate?

To circumnavigate some of these obstacles I choose the partners, to the extent possible putting boys with girls and separating best friends. To avoid negotiation and whining, I put sticky notes indicating who sits where on the paired desks before class. After a few moments of confusion, students settle into these somewhat uncomfortable new seats. The unease is an important part of this process. I want students to behave in ways that are outside their conventional repertoire. I want them to be more than their typical funny, wacky, goofy, and carefree selves. I want them to behave like writers.

I then tell students to talk to their partners for five minutes about anything apart from this class and their assignment. Even students who have together attended the same schools since kindergarten may find this an uneasy moment. Teenagers tend to run in packs and talk with the same small group of friends day after day. Suddenly they are being urged to establish a new relationship on strange ground. But most students—although they are reluctant to show it at first—welcome the opportunity. As they talk, I return drafts to the original writers and then have them follow these instructions. It always seems to work best for me to conduct students through this process step-by-step rather than handing out a worksheet for them to follow. This makes it harder to race through the steps, easier not to feel a fool for attending to each task.

1. Ask students to read through their own draft silently, stopping after every paragraph to write one question in the margin that they would like their partner to answer. I model on the board the kind of questions they might pose: Is my first paragraph irredeemably boring? Can you tell what this paper is going to be about? Is this example apt? Is this quotation too long? Can you think of anything else I could say here? Does this sentence make sense to you? Do you understand this point? What should I do to connect these ideas? Is this irrelevant? It may be important to tell students that you will be collecting these annotated drafts and giving them credit for the quality of the questions they posed.

2. Then ask students to read aloud their drafts to their partners, stopping after each paragraph to ask their question. As their partner responds, the writer should take note of suggestions or

further questions. You will need to circulate around the room during this step. Often when a partner can't answer a question the pair will look to the teacher for help. Rather than considering this a weakness of their work together, I see it as progress because their questions are focused on a particular issue and are not merely a vague cry for support.

3. Once the first writer has finished reading, repeat the process for the partner.

4. Before the period ends, draw the class together to discuss what they have just done. Students need to be reminded of the purpose of such work together. Try to draw from them what they have garnered from their partner's feedback and how this will be useful as they revise.

5. Make the final copy of the paper due the next day. Feedback cools quickly. If students wait three days to revise, they are likely to have forgotten what their partner suggested. Their notes will have become too cryptic to be deciphered and the day will have been wasted. You can always make exceptions for students who have a big math test to study for or a basketball game that night. Better to push those who can knuckle down immediately to the task of rewriting.

This process may seem extremely directive to readers who prefer a discovery approach to writing. While I acknowledge that some students blossom in a looser environment, in my experience most of these writers are already thriving. It's the students who are wilting, unable or unwilling to tap the nutrients within themselves, for whom I structure such lessons. These teenagers need a teacher to walk them step-by-step through a series of lessons that will produce a negotiable product. As Lisa Delpit writes in *Other People's Children* (1995)

Although the problem is not necessarily inherent in the method, in some instances adherents of process approaches to writing create situations in which students ultimately find themselves held accountable for knowing a set of rules about which no one has ever directly informed them. Teachers do students no service to suggest, even implicitly, that "product" is not important. In this country students will be judged on their product regardless of the process they utilized to achieve it. And that product, based as it is on the specific codes of a particular culture, is more readily produced when the directives of how to produce it are made explicit.

If such explicitness is not provided to students, what it feels like to people who are old enough to judge is that there are secrets being kept, that time is being wasted, that the teacher is abdicating his or her duty to teach. (31)

As students respond to a peer's draft under the tutelage of a guiding teacher, they begin to see the importance of clear communication. They discover that they do know the difference between incoherent and coherent writing. Though struggling writers are rarely able to help one another with editing, they can offer powerful feedback, particularly when their response is oral rather than written, to another student's paper. Without the structure, too many students rush though peer assessment, checking boxes at random on the worksheet, giving little more than cursory attention to the task. Within the structure students learn a method for thinking about revision. If a draft is not communicating clearly to a peer, it is unlikely to be a satisfactory product for a wider audience.

Self-Assessment Strategies

I am increasingly persuaded that students most need, vitally need, to acquire the ability to assess their work for themselves. As long as they feel that only a teacher is capable of telling them whether the paper they have turned in is good, they will be insecure writers, incapable of improvement. Students should know themselves whether the paper they turn in is an A, B, or C essay. To acquire this confidence they need to be put through the paces of evaluating their own work through a teacher's lens. This is more than simply an editing skill—though editing will contribute to the final grade. Students need to grasp for themselves the evaluative criteria that readers use when determining whether a piece of writing has value.

The importance of self-assessment was brought home to me one evening when my son called from college. The conversation went something like this:

Me: Hi, James. How're you doing?

James: Hey, Mom. I'm great. I've got a term paper due tomorrow morning, but I'm good.

Me (*yuppie-teacher mom, overeager to help her freshman son do well*): Why don't you email me the paper so I can proofread it before you have to turn it in?

James: Uh, well, I haven't exactly written anything yet but don't worry, I've done all the reading.

The paper was due a short ten hours from the time we spoke, yet James had no doubt that he could write the seven pages. Clearly the essay would have been better had he begun working earlier and set aside more time for revision and reflection, but given the first-year lifestyle of many college students, I don't think James' work habits are uncommon. The professor was willing to give students feedback on their drafts, but James was "too busy" to avail himself of the offer. He was depending on the skills he had acquired in high school to enable him to produce a piece of writing under pressure and with little assistance from anyone but himself and a spell-check program.

The conversation with James—who, by the way, received a B on the paper and learned the hard way that letting a professor vet your thesis is always a good idea—inspired me to think about how I could build students' self-assessment skills. I developed the following set of guidelines for leading students through the process. As with the peer-response lesson, I do not hand students this list but rather walk them through each step. All students need to begin is a draft and a highlighter.

- Highlight the first sentence of your essay. Does it compel a reader's attention? Does it include the hackneyed phrase "this story is about"? Make a note in the margin to return to this important opening sentence.

- Highlight the last sentence of your introductory paragraph and the first sentence of your initial supporting paragraph. Is there a transition? If not, write: "Needs a transition word or phrase" in the margin. (Note to teacher: Remind students of transitional expressions, listing them on the board.)

- Draw a line at the end of every sentence. Are most of your sentences three to four lines long? Are most of your sentences three to four words long? Is there variety in your sentence structures?

- Scan your essay for RIP (rest in peace) words: different, really, a lot, great, awesome, very, get, amazing, incredible. Cross out every one. (Note to teacher: Suggest alternatives to these overworn words. For example: "Different" is survived by unique, startling, surprising, remarkable, curious, etc.) and there is always a more precise verb than "get."

- Highlight all adverbs. An easy way to do this is to search for words that end in "ly." Try to replace them with stronger verbs and more powerful adjectives.

- Check sentence openings. Circle any sentence that begins with "There is/are/were." Scan to see if you have a series of sentences that all begin with "He" or "She" or "I." Make a note in the margin to rewrite these sentences.

- Circle all contractions. Spell them out. (Note to teacher: Contractions lend a conversational tone to writing. Students often have difficulty adopting a more formal tone for broader audiences. Eliminating contractions is one way to help them develop a sense of how to achieve this.)

- Examine your conclusion. Don't begin with "Finally," "In conclusion," or "Thus." Does your conclusion explore the significance of your thesis? Ask yourself, "Why does what I have written matter?"

This self-assessment exercise can take up to forty-five minutes to complete. Students who put effort into the work tell me that it has helped them learn how to think about revision. Often, dutiful students feel cheated when they invest care peer-editing another student's essay and only to receive smiley faces and "Good job!" comments in return. Here writers reap what they sow.

The Sweet Sixteen

You know good writing when you read it. Many of your students may not. In an effort to be more explicit about the features of effective writing, my colleague Rob Thais created what he called "The Sweet Sixteen." These descriptors have many classroom applications, but I find them most useful for reminding students what they are aiming for.

These Sweet Sixteen guidelines not only provide students with a framework for self-assessment, they also help to remind me about what to applaud and what to suggest in student drafts. When Alice Ollstein sent me the following draft of an essay she was writing for the California Association of Teachers of English creative writing contest for students, I considered what she wrote through this lens. Alice was writing to the following prompt:

The Power of One

Sometimes one person can make a significant difference in your life or in the lives of those around you. Bryce Courtenay wrote a book called *The Power of One*. It is about a young boy who finds the strength within himself to change his life and to do what is right. But he has help from special individuals along the way. Think about the people who have made an impact or positive difference in your life: a member of your family, a teacher, a friend, a coach, or a classmate. Write a poem, short story, or personal narrative about the power of one person in your life.

Below is an email exchange I had with Alice on her essay. We had talked briefly the day before about her first draft. Though full of engaging detail what she had written was lacking in what The Sweet Sixteen refers to as unity.

On Nov 25, 2004, at 8:19 AM, CaptainAliceO@netscape.net wrote:

Here's a 2nd draft of my piece about rabbi neil. I think it could still be better, but this is an improvement. are my changes/additions good? what else does it need?
thank you so much, Alice

Ideas

1. **Unity:** You have one clear thesis that responds to the assigned task, and all the ideas in your essay help to support that thesis.
2. **Insight:** Your ideas are thoughtful and stimulating, yet reasonable and true to the material.
3. **Argument:** You prove your ideas clearly, logically, and completely. You fully prepare the reader to understand each sentence and its purpose in your paper.
4. **Evidence:** The quality and quantity of evidence strongly supports your ideas and shows thorough knowledge of the material.

Organization

5. **Introduction:** Your first paragraph engages the reader and introduces a clear thesis or purpose.
6. **Paragraphing:** Each body paragraph sticks to one idea, and each idea is discussed in only one body paragraph.
7. **Flow:** Your main ideas are presented in a logical and effective order, made clear via topic sentences, paragraph conclusions, and transitions.
8. **Conclusion:** You conclude with a graceful reminder of your thesis.

Style

9. **Conciseness:** You express ideas simply and clearly without wasted words or unnecessary repetition.
10. **Vocabulary:** Your choice of words is interesting and precise but not pretentious.
11. **Sentence Structure:** Your sentences are strong, graceful, and suitably varied in length and structure.
12. **Vividness:** You enliven your writing with concrete language, fresh and specific detail, and metaphor without cliché.

Grammar

13. **Sentence Sense:** Your writing is free of run-on sentences and fragments.
14. **Grammar and Usage:** You follow the rules of Standard English.
15. **Mechanics:** Your spelling, capitalization, and punctuation are accurate.
16. **Format:** You follow the conventions of documentation.

In a world where faith is a faux pas, one man has instilled within me a passion for being Jewish, and a desire to improve the world. If this man, Rabbi Neil Comess-Daniels, were to rip his tie and dress-shirt from his chest to reveal a blazing shin (a Hebrew letter that would clearly stand for Superjew) it would not surprise me very much. Throughout my life, has displayed such extraordinary powers of kindness, understanding, and spirit, that I decided long ago that he couldn't possibly be a human being. He is, obviously, a Super Jew.

Eight days after I came into the world, I participated in my first Jewish tradition: my own bris, or baby naming. Rabbi Neil Comess-Daniels conducted the ceremony, and all progressed beautifully until I interrupted his poetic words with a large belch. The assembled guests politely tittered as my family blushed and squirmed in their seats. "Look," Neil gestured towards my chubby, mischevious grin. "She's expressing herself already!" Ever since that day, Rabbi Neil has encouraged me not only to express myself, but to get excited about my faith, and take an active role in social change.

Neil has played a role in every major event of my life. He held me in his arms and said blessings over my squirming, burping form at my baby-naming. He stood under the chuppa at my mother and step-father's wedding, chanting Hebrew prayers as I scattered rose petals. He sat by my side as I poured over dense texts of Hebrew and tried to find a connection between ancient laws of animal sacrifice and my bat-mitzvah. He sat by me as I clutched my notepad to my chest and anxiously presented my views on the homeless crisis to Congressman Henry Waxman. Without his super-human support, I could have never accomplished what I have.

Beginning with "Rabbi and Me" classes, where my fellow toddlers and I wiggled across the dance floor while Neil played Hebrew folk songs on his banjo, and culminating in confirmation class, where we studied other religions and participated in interfaith events to promote tolerance, Neil taught me about my faith in an engaging, inspiring way. After spending thirteen years learning the language, values and history of our people, the tenth grade confirmation class, under Neil's direction, set out to apply what we learned to modern times. We flew to Washington D.C. and met with temples from across the country to debate such issues as gay marrige, capital punishment and the Patriot Act. At once we had both the Torah and the Constitution at our fingertips, and we jumped between them, citing Leviticus and Bill of Rights with equal ease. Neil taught me what it means to be an American Jew. Through this, I came to understand that the Jewish people have a set of values that has survived thousands of years, influencing people all over the world and holding strong in times of crisis. Once carved onto stone tablets, they are carved just as deeply and permanently in my mind. Thanks to Neil, I know that being a Jew means taking these ancient values and applying them to our modern world. The government, once something so cold and intangible to me that I never bothered in keeping up with the news of its inner workings, is now alive and within my reach. As Neil led my friends and I up Capitol Hill and into the office of our Congressman, I felt for the first time that even though I am only a little girl from Santa Monica, I have the power to change the world.

Knowing full well that my friends and I were eager to show off, Neil called upon us to make up a skit promoting the temple's canned food drive to the kindergarden class. He knew this would hold the attention of a six year old far more than a simple announcement would. We came up with our own superhero, called Super Jew. Sporting spandex and payas, he flew around the world giving challah to the hungry, tzedakah to the poor and ruach, or spirit, to the down-trodden. My classmates selected me to play Super Jew. Proud, but nervous to fill Superjew's large shoes, I let my friends scotch-tape a construction paper shin to my chest, tie a sweatshirt around my neck in imitation of a cape, and pin a yarmulke to my tangle of blonde curls. I stood outside the classroom, ear pressed to the door, as I listened to my friends perform the beginning of our skit. Wrapped in trash bag, they moaned and sighed: "We are SO hungry! There's nothing to eat! If only someone would save us!"

"Look!" my friend Sammy cried. "Up in the sky!"

"It's a bird!"

"It's a plane!"

"It's a . . . rabbi?"

I burst through the door, a can of peas in each fist, and stood with my hands on my hips, beaming out over the sea of eager faces. "Hi kids, I'm SuperJew. I fly around using my Jewish powers to save the world, but I need your help. Who wants to help me save the world?" A forest of hands shot up. I saw Neil beaming at me out of the corner of my eye. I felt a rush of pride, and continued with gusto.

"Well, it's easy! Just ask your mommy or daddy to donate some canned goods to the temple's food drive, and we'll get them into the tummies of hungry people. Like this!" With a flourish, I presented a can of peas to my trash-bag wrapped friends, who mimed eating its contents. "We're so not hungry anymore!" my friends cried. "Thanks, SuperJew!" The audience cheered and clapped, none louder or longer than Neil. "You're welcome, good people. I must go now to save others!" I spread my arms and flew out of the classroom.

Out in the hallway, Neil put a hand on my shoulder. "Fabulous skit! You make a great SuperJew." I looked down at the sagging paper shin on my chest, which, away from the applause and bravado of the skit, looked like a poor excuse for a superhero's symbol. "You're the real SuperJew," I told him. I thought of the hundreds of people that listen, breathless to his stirring sermons. I thought of the homeless people that he helps. I thought of the hundreds of students that he teaches to be good Jews, but more importantly, good human beings. "You actually go around saving the world."

He laughed. "There's nothing preventing you from saving the world too." He said, and walked down the hall, leaving me alone with my thoughts. Ever since that day, not only has Neil encouraged me to "save the world," as I so passionately desired to, he has provided original and meaningful opportunities to do so. With his direction, I've led a Shabbat service and played my clarinet at a retirement home, attended political rallies for causes I believe in, lobbied my congressman, and shared a meal with the homeless community. I want to thank Neil for helping me discover my inner SuperJew. I can't wait to don my cape and go out to save the world.

On Nov 25, 2004, at 12:06 PM, Carol Jago wrote:

Hi, Alice.
Terrific revision. Here are a few more places in the essay you might want to think about:

- This opening is much more targeted to the contest's prompt. I think this is an excellent idea. What about including an "often"—"where faith is often a faux pas." I love the phrase and your point but worry it is too much of an overstatement.

- Why would the letter "clearly" stand for SuperJew? Maybe eliminate the adverb. Also I'd use a long dash rather than parenthesis. This will make your point less of an aside. Be sure your capitalization of SuperJew is consistent throughout.
- No need for a "large" before "belch." The noun says it all.
- Just a suggestion here—I'm not sure if I agree with myself—what about toward the end of your essay where you write "super-human support" say Super-Jew support? It might be overdoing things, though.
- "Knowing full well" is a cliché. What I like is that it suggests how well and deeply he knows you all. Think about how you can say this without the worn phrase.
- The final sentence could be improved by replacing "I can't wait" with something more concrete and less common. "It's my turn now?" You'll come up with something.

This is delightful, Alice. I love the dialogue toward the end and the lighthearted tone throughout.

Mrs. J

You will notice the tentative nature of my response to Alice's draft. Alice may be only sixteen years old, but she has already become an accomplished writer who has learned, adapted, and applied much of what The Sweet Sixteen describes. I don't want to suggest by word or deed that mine is the last word in her writing. Every revision decision should be hers.

SIX

Alternatives to Essays

Sometimes the best way to handle the paper load is not to assign essays in the first place. Clearly I don't mean never assigning papers, but if the primary goal is to measure whether students have read and comprehended a novel or play—and if you are recovering from reading the last set of papers—it might make sense to consider alternatives to the traditional analytical essay. Along with offering respite for the teacher, such assignments also allow struggling writers an opportunity to demonstrate that they have done the work and understood the text without being penalized for their limited writing skills. Essays are not the only way to measure literary understanding. I think of Hannah, an avid reader and keen student who often had her hand up in class and, more to the point, always had something thoughtful to say. Reading Hannah's papers I felt let down. They never reflected the depth of thinking of which I knew she was capable. The prose was infantile and full of sweeping generalizations supported by long quotations bereft of accompanying analysis. A generous B– was the best grade she ever earned. By offering students alternative ways to show what they know, I gave myself some breathing space and students the opportunity to respond to text creatively.

Expert Group Reports

At the conclusion of our reading of Seamus Heaney's translation of *Beowulf*, I divided the class into six groups and asked each group to suggest and research a topic that could deepen their understanding of the epic poem. I provided them with materials I had collected over the years on the subjects and invited students to use the classroom computers for Internet sources. They explored:

- the role of the hero
- the role of the monster
- songs and storytelling
- armor, jewelry, and gift giving
- the mead hall
- dragons in literature

Their task was to become experts on the topic and present their findings to the class. I discouraged enactments and instead urged students to teach us what they had learned. They were given one class period for research and on the second day we began their presentations. The results were often remarkable tours de force that resulted in deeper understanding for the entire class. The group that researched the mead hall included students who had been confused by my comparison of Hrothgar's hall with Camelot and were surprised to discover the more primitive, barnlike architectural structure Grendel raided. They copied the image they found on a website onto poster board and beamed with pride when I asked if I could save it to use with next year's class.

Another expert group assignment that works well is to construct a list of challenging discussion questions and assign trios of students to direct a class discussion around this issue. At the conclusion of my twelfth graders' reading of *Crime and Punishment* I put students into small groups, distributing the strongest readers and assigning the hardest questions to trios who needed the challenge. I told students that their grade would depend on the quality of the classroom conversation that they generated. In order to be successful, students had to identify supporting passages, design follow-up questions, and become "experts" on their topic.

1. Why do so many important scenes in *Crime and Punishment* take place in confined spaces and hallways?

72

2. What is the significance of the biblical story of Lazarus that Raskolnikov and Sonia read together?
3. How does *Crime and Punishment* compare with more traditional detective stories and Porfiry with classic detectives?
4. What do you make of the scenes at the river? What does the water represent to Raskolnikov at various points in the story?
5. Why do you think Raskolnikov displays so much incompetence in his execution of the grand robbery?
6. Razumihin's name means "reason" in Russian. How does this character serve as a foil to Raskolnikov?
7. What do you make of the fact that Dounia chose not to shoot the evil Svidrigailov?
8. What role does drunkenness play throughout Dostoyevski's narrative?
9. Do you think the epilogue is a concession to readers looking for a happy ending or is it an essential part of the total story?

The group presentations have no time limit, and the class discussions may range over several days. I enter into the conversation wholeheartedly, filling in blanks when a group is insufficiently prepared or may have missed an important point. I also raise questions that continue to puzzle me as a reader. The "experts" don't always know either, but as they posit possible explanations, their ability to analyze improves. I want to teach students to probe a text, not mine it for easy answers.

The unique feature of this expert group assignment does not consist in the questions. Teachers have long relied on study questions and appropriate issues for any commonly taught novel can easily be located through the Google search engine. What is different is the "divide and conquer" approach. While asking students to write out answers individually may ensure that each student grapples alone with each question, it also encourages them to copy from each other's work. In addition, the collected papers create a cross for the teacher's back.

Research Without the Papers

Almost all state standards documents require students to conduct research, often beginning in the early grades. The American Diploma Project sets the following research benchmarks for all high school graduates.

While I have argued long and hard that research is most authentically positioned in content area classes such as science and social studies, responsibility for this arguably literary standard continues to fall inexorably on the backs of English teachers. One way to help students meet these standards without taking home a stack of term papers two feet high is to ask students to work through the research process and present their findings to one another. I continue to require my tenth-grade students to write a literary research paper in the spring (which I describe in *Cohesive Writing* [2002]), but several times throughout the school year I ask students to do research that does not culminate in a five- to seven-page paper.

Research/Problem-Solving Skills

Conceive, plan, and complete simple and complex research projects designed to address specific questions and/or solve problems by:

- defining and narrowing a problem or research topic;
- gathering relevant information from a variety of print and electronic sources, as well as from direct observation, interviews, and surveys;
- organizing information collected by taking notes, outlining ideas, paraphrasing information, and making charts, conceptual maps, learning logs, and time lines;
- evaluating the credibility and usefulness of resources (including online resources), making distinctions about their relative value and significance for the project;
- conveying information and ideas from primary and secondary sources accurately and coherently;
- documenting quotations, paraphrases, and other information using a standard format; and
- reporting findings within prescribed time and/or length requirements, as appropriate.

A few years ago a group of African American students approached me in early February to ask what we would be doing for Black History Month. In truth, I had planned a unit on point of view in short stories, but went home that night knowing I needed to think again. I went to my computer and devised the following mini–research project for the class.

Researching African American Poets

Your task: to research and report to the class on the life and work of an African American poet. Please check with me after you choose and before embarking on your research. Here is a list of possible poets to give you some ideas. Be sure to select a poet whose poems you enjoy.

- Rita Dove
- Paul Laurence Dunbar
- Nikki Giovanni
- Maya Angelou
- Paul Beatty
- Alice Walker
- Grace Nichols
- Sonya Sanchez
- Angela Johnson
- Sapphire
- Quincy Troupe
- Lucille Clifton
- Countee Cullen
- Jackie Kaye

1. Find three poems you like by the poet you have chosen.
2. Research the poet's life and the times.
3. Prepare a five-minute presentation to the class on your poet including a memorized performance of one of the poems (or portion of a long poem).

Hand in:

- a title page
- copies of the three poems
- the notes for you presentation

You will note that Langston Hughes was not on my list of recommended poets. This is the one African American poet students are exposed to most often in school. I want to broaden their horizons. Students almost always ask if they can use hip-hop artists for this project. I try to steer them toward more literary choices. The assignment works well as an individual or paired student project. One advantage of having students working in pairs is that it results in half as many presentations. Neither option results in a stack of papers clamoring to be read.

Responses in Verse

In *With Rigor for All* (2000) I describe a lesson employing Wallace Stevens' "Thirteen Ways of Looking at a Blackbird" as a model for having students write a poem in which they enumerate thirteen interpretations of the character of Lady Macbeth, Paul in *All Quiet on the Western Front*, Mersault in *The Stranger*, Holden Caufield in *The Catcher in the Rye*, or Brutus in *Julius Caesar*. I also use a poem by Sandra Cisneros called "Abuelito Who" as an alternative to character analysis essays. The poet lists a series of concrete images to describe her grandfather, surprising metaphors like "who is dough and feathers / who is a watch and a glass of water." We read and discuss the poem, noting the power of a catalogue to re-create a character in the mind's eye. Immediately following this discussion, I ask students to use "Abuelito Who" to write a poem that analyzes a main character from Mary Shelley's *Frankenstein*. The instructions are simple:

1. Choose a character.
2. Make a list of objects and images associated with this character.
3. Using "Abuelito Who" as a model, write a poem about this character.
4. Be sure that the poem conveys the character's most essential traits.
5. Revise and type the poem for display.

I invite students to compose their poetic imitations in class and, before the end of the period, I ask a few volunteers to read their imitations aloud to one another. This always seems to help those who have had difficulty with the assignment to see how easy the task is. At home they revise and type the poems, and on the following day I display their products on the bulletin board. With Sandra Cisneros' cadences as a model, Hanna Schneider wrote the following poem to demonstrate her understanding of Victor Frankenstein. The poem displays a level of sophistication that Hanna has yet to master in prose.

Victor Frankenstein Who

Victor Frankenstein who works in the lab all night
and asks why not create life
who is books and body parts
who is a lightening rod and a stormy night
whose hair is all sparks
is too terrified to think today
who tells Elizabeth you are my diamond
who tells her she is my love
whose heart is broken
can't undo what he has made
lies awake in his little room all night and day
who used to laugh in the sunshine
is obsessed
is a scientist gone mad
is scared shut the door
doesn't live here anymore
is hiding in the storm
who talks to me inside my head
is running after his creation and chasing his dream
who haunts laboratories and genetic engineers
who still lives
asking who loves him
and why, why?

—*Hanna Schneider*

It is easy to tell that Hanna read *Frankenstein* with care and fully understood Mary Shelley's hero. The assignment allowed her to shine. It is also easier for a teacher to read a set of poems than a set of character analysis essays. Bill Burns, a colleague of mine from the Irvine Writing Project, used a similar assignment with his twelfth graders who were reading Sophocles' *Antigone*. Overwhelmed by their essays—he meets 180 students a day—Bill asked his students to write two-stanza choral odes with the first strophe a summarization of the action in the play and the second antistrophe a commentary on the action. One of the things I like best about poetic imitation is that by walking in the poet's footsteps students come to know the original poem more deeply and begin to understand how a poet employs rhythm, syntax, imagery, and diction. I don't try to assign evaluative grades to these creative endeavors and instead give As for effort.

A caveat is in order. Creative responses should not replace traditional literary analysis essays. I will always remember an exchange I witnessed during one semester when a colleague used my classroom during my preparation period. "Ladies and gentlemen, your papers are due. Please pass them forward." As the essays on *Julius Caesar* that students had been working on for weeks surged toward the teacher's desk, one young man leaned back in his chair, arms crossed, obviously paperless. The instructor turned to him and politely inquired as to the whereabouts of his work.

"I don't do essays" was the boy's response.

He doesn't "do" essays? Although I was a mere accidental observer of this exchange, I was livid. In a high school English class, writing essays is not an optional activity. I was upset that this student felt entirely within his rights to declare that he had no intention of devoting any time whatsoever to the assignment. Should he earn a passing grade in the class? Should the teacher design alternative avenues for this student to demonstrate what he knows about Shakespeare? I used to think that he should but I have changed my mind. A corollary of the right to free public education is the responsibility to complete the work assigned. Of course teachers should provide support for struggling students and offer them many different ways of acquiring basic skills. Of course we want to furnish extra academic assistance for children who for a variety of reasons are unable to find help at home. But the lowering of expectations of student performance beyond all recognition is of no conceivable benefit to the student. Moreover, by allowing students to slip through school, awarding credit to students who write almost nothing, a teacher is guilty of educational malpractice.

Motivating Students

Business managers know that the strength of any successful company is directly related to the well-being of its employees. They understand that dollars invested in organizing incentive programs and creating career paths give a return in terms of productivity. Astute employers invite workers' suggestions as to how a particular job might be performed more efficiently. They do so because they realize that disgruntled, discontented, disappointed, disillusioned employees are seldom productive. Furious workers make faulty widgets.

Students are a lot like employees. Required to dedicate a specified number of hours, a contractual "shift" for which they receive grades as recompense, students tend to develop a hatred of their "job" and resentment toward their "boss." They seek out ways to survive their "shift," the school day, with the barest minimum of effort; they see little or no return for individual initiative and yearn for Friday, payday, to roll around. Teachers could learn a great deal from management research. For example, a common misconception in many professions is that money is the best motivator. While a salary raise is always welcome, it often achieves little except the increase of overhead costs. Motivating human beings is more complex than the simple exchange of dollars for work, compensation for time expended. Companies with exemplary production records often point to factors like trust and praise and job responsibility as having more influence on output than monetary rewards. The ability to exercise control over their working lives is another powerful influence on production. A majority of the employees of Southwest Airlines identify having fun on the job as a vital motivator. In similar fashion, the promise of an A or the threat of an F rarely, by itself, motivates students. Neither do pep talks. In my experience, chiding teenagers to "do their best" and "work to their potential" or "just try harder" is a waste of a teacher's breath. Even the most dynamic exhortations achieve little more than a momentary squall in the classroom air.

Another lesson that can be learned from industry involves work that has been simplified to the point that it becomes meaningless. It is congruent with human approaches to tasks and, therefore, good teaching practice to break down a difficult assignment into its component parts. In theory, as students work through the required steps, they acquire the skills needed to complete the larger assignment. In practice, however, the completion of the assignment can be indefinitely prorogued. As a friend of mine described his years in school: "practicing, practicing, practicing for a day that never came."

The mornings on which I wake up excited about the work ahead are almost always days when I plan to try something new. What motivates me is the challenge of applying fresh solutions to old problems. Students are no different. If teachers treat them like wage-slaves working for grades, they will behave as such. To encourage self-motivated learning,

- Give students responsibility.
- Trust them.
- Listen to them.
- Observe them as they write.
- Solve problems together.
- Express confidence in students' ability to write well.
- Praise them for diligent effort.
- Celebrate their ideas.
- Support them with approval, coaching, feedback, and encouragement.

I know this sounds like common sense, but maybe we could use a bit more common sense in education. For example: in the debate over how schools should be improved teachers, administrators, legislators, and parents have made clear what they want and don't want to see happen. But an important voice is often missing—students'. Public Agenda, a nonprofit, nonpartisan research organization, conducted a nationwide telephone survey of over 1,300 high school students. *Getting By: What American Teenagers Really Think About Their Schools* (1997) reports that:

1. Most American teenagers say they believe that "getting an education" is essential to their future. They would like to do well in school and go on to college.

2. Most teenagers do not actively dislike their schools, but many see serious shortcomings—too many disruptive students, poor discipline, crowded classes. Private-school students have fewer such complaints.
3. Most teenagers see little reason to study academic subjects such as history, science, and literature. They view most of what they learn—apart from "the basics"—as tedious and irrelevant.
4. Most youngsters readily admit they don't work as hard as they could in school. They say higher standards would make them do more.
5. Most teenagers say that the close and unwavering attention of teachers, even more than higher standards, is the real key to getting them to learn more.
6. Youngsters expect a lot from their teachers and have very clear ideas of what constitutes a "good" or "bad" teacher. Private-school youngsters have far more positive views about their teachers.
7. Students and teachers in public schools complain of a lack of respect and civility, and students make some serious charges about the behavior of their peers and the social scene they inhabit.
8. African American and Hispanic teens support higher standards for all youngsters but are more critical of their schools. African American youngsters, in particular, believe in the benefits of education and academic accomplishments.
9. Private-school students are significantly more positive about their schools and teachers than are youngsters in public school. They say they thrive in a more structured atmosphere.

You may wonder whether the young people polled actually know enough to have useful opinions. Should a collection of idiosyncratic teenage experiences, colored as they are by adolescent attitudes and raging hormones, affect public policy? I think so. No rational manufacturer would ignore such broad-based customer dissatisfaction with his product. No responsible service provider would discount such clear recommendations for what clients feel they need. High school students have spent over a decade in desks and their experience of the classroom is current. Students have earned the right to be heard.

The most interesting thing about this report is that the views of these young people do not match any particular ideological agenda for educational reform. Those who are looking for evidence that the primary difficulty schools face is a lack of resources will find support in students' criticism of crowded classrooms and tattered textbooks. Those who seek proof that what America needs are higher standards will find comfort here too.

In her closing comment Deborah Wadsworth, executive director of Public Agenda, states, "America's teenagers are calling out for help. They are telling us something we should already know—that by asking for less, we get less. If we ask for more, on the other hand, they will respond. Perhaps these teenagers are merely marking time until we adults show that we value academic achievement and civil and ethical behavior as much as we value celebrity status, athletic prowess, or financial success" (Public Agenda 1997).

Lives on the Boundary

Anyone familiar with the writer Mike Rose would know better than to look for him in the spotlight. Combing a crowded room for the author, you would be most likely to find him in a quiet corner— watching, listening, waiting to talk with you. His gentle spirit both encourages confidences and invites reflection. This same spirit animates his book *Lives on the Boundary* (1999). Rose invites readers to accompany him on the journey he made toward understanding how a country so full of promise could create an educational underclass. Part memoir, part theory, it is a classic in the progressive canon.

Lives on the Boundary interweaves the story of the author's own experience growing up in Los Angeles with those of his similarly alienated and unprepared students. I wish I could report that in the decade since its publication his book triggered so many epiphanies in so many educators that the problem has been solved. Unfortunately, academic achievement in urban schools suggests otherwise. All too many of our young people's lives remain stuck on the boundary.

The book's preface explains that "(t)his is a hopeful book about those who fail. It is a book about the abilities hidden by class and cultural barriers. And it is a book about movement: about what happens as people who have failed begin to participate in the educational system that has seemed so harsh and distant to them." I find it takes a great deal of courage to sustain hope for progressive change in a political climate where mandates for punitive responses to underachievement have become the norm.

In every state in the Union local and state governing bodies are holding students accountable for rigorous academic standards in writing. The American Diploma Project has the following benchmarks for graduating high school seniors.

Analysis of Arguments

The graduating high school senior can:

Identify an author's point of view and describe his attitude toward the topic.

Distinguish among facts, supported inferences, and unsupported opinions in texts.

Distinguish various types of arguments, including arguments by causation, analogy, authority, emotion, and logic.

Evaluate the validity of an argument by analyzing the effectiveness of its logical structure and the rhetorical devices used to support claims or assertions.

Evaluate the validity of an argument by comparing its assertions with evidence available from other sources.

Identify unsupported inferences, false assumptions, bias, propaganda, or fallacious reasoning (e.g., circular reasoning, false causality, overgeneralization, oversimplification, self-contradiction, attack ad hominem, appeal to authority or emotion, and bandwagoning).

Adjudicate contradictions presented within and/or across expository texts (e.g., contradictory claims, conflicting arguments).

On one level this is a good thing. Our vision of democracy depends on a literate populace. But the popularity of this idea among voters has turned the standards movement into a battle cry: Higher Scores! Harder Classes! More Homework! Mike Rose debunked these myths years ago. "We live, in America, with so many platitudes about motivation and self-

Writing and Speaking

The graduating high school senior can:

Demonstrate control of Standard English through the correct use of grammar and mechanics in written and oral work.

Select the use of language appropriate for the purpose, audience, and context of the work, including Standard English for clarity; technical language for specificity; and non–Standard English for rhetorical effect.

Write and speak in simple, compound, and compound-complex sentences with effective coordination and subordination of ideas to express complete thoughts (e.g., parallel structures, major phrasal and clausal constituents, modifiers).

Demonstrate knowledge of the principles of composition, such as paragraphing, smooth transitions, and variety in sentence structure.

Formulate valid written and oral arguments according to the conventions of different modes (narrative, persuasive, expository) that:

- convey a clear and concise thesis statement;
- exhibit a logical structure appropriate to the audience and purpose;
- rely on accurate assumptions;
- group related ideas and maintain a consistent focus;
- make valid inferences;
- support judgments through the effective use of evidence and well-chosen details;
- make effective use of rhetorical devices;
- provide a coherent conclusion; and
- (*for presentations*) employ proper eye contact, speaking rate, volume, enunciation, inflection, and gestures to communicate ideas effectively.

Produce work-related text (e.g., résumés, bios, job applications, directions, instructions, work orders, memos, correspondence, briefs) or make oral presentations according to conventional styles, that:

- address audience needs, stated purpose, and context, including relevant information and excluding extraneous information;
- anticipate and address potential counterclaims and misunderstandings;
- make use of appropriate strategies, such as creating a visual hierarchy, using white space and graphics as appropriate; and
- include proper salutation, closing, and signature.

reliance and individualism—and myths spun from them, like those of Horatio Alger—that we find it hard to accept the fact that they are serious nonsense. To live your early life on the streets of South L.A.— or Homewood or Spanish Harlem or Chicago's South Side or any one of hundreds of other depressed communities—and to journey up through the top levels of the American educational system will call for support and guidance at many, many points along the way." Voters and legislators need to hear this. So do educational leaders. Until and unless we provide support and guidance to every student in the public school system, America will continue to be home to a huge educational underclass.

As Mike Rose explained, "There is much talk these days about the value of a classical humanistic education, a call for an immersion in the humanities, a return to great books. These appeals raise lots of suspicions, for such curricula have traditionally served to exclude working-class people from the classroom. It doesn't, of necessity, have to be that way. The teachers that fate sent my way worked at making the humanities truly human." Rereading these words, I develop goose bumps. This is the kind of teacher I try to be, guiding reluctant scholars to express themselves articulately, helping them when they falter and cheering when they succeed.

Shouting "Higher! Harder! More!" is never going to raise academic standards for students like Mike Rose. What it will take is determined leadership committed to real student achievement. Rose warned that focusing on quantification—on errors we can quantify, on test scores we can rank—will divert us from rather than guide us toward solutions. "Numbers seduce us into thinking we know more than we do; they give the false assurance of rigor but reveal little about the complex cognitive and emotional processes behind the tally of errors and wrong answers." In the current political climate, where standardized test scores are the measure of both teaching and learning, we have never needed such guidance more. Mike Rose, the quiet man in the corner, still has much to say to us.

I firmly believe that effective writing instruction can make a difference for students whose lives are on the boundary.

SEVEN

Uncommon Sense for Handling the Paper Load

How would it feel to learn that, after all the time you spent grading papers, students had not bothered to read your comments? Given that at this very moment seventy-six student essays sit in a stack beside me, crying out to be read, this is a question of extreme personal relevance. Two Canadian researchers, Joe Belanger and Philip Allingham, interviewed high school students immediately after the students' graded essays were returned to them. The goal of the research was to discover how students responded to the grades, comments, and criticisms teachers offered on their compositions. Warning: the following results will depress you.

Belanger and Allingham (2002) found that while students were extremely interested in finding out their grades, their reaction to the grade distracted students from the kind of improvement that might be triggered by teacher comments. "Many students who received the grade they expected did not read any of the teachers' comments despite the fact that teachers had made a number of suggestions students could apply to future essays" (2). Students who received a grade higher than what they expected spent time "basking in the warmth of the occasion . . . lingering on any praise they found" (3), but did nothing to try to figure out why the grade was better than expected. Most disturbing of all, students who received a grade much lower than expected did not read teacher comments either. These students were often highly agitated and focused on ways to persuade the teacher to let them rewrite the paper for a higher grade. One would assume that if students were allowed to rewrite that they would—finally—cast an eye over what the teacher suggested for improvement. Belanger and Allingham found no evidence to suggest that students who do not revise read teacher comments at all. Students' responses to their teachers' comments were peripherally pragmatic and grade oriented.

Do Teacher Comments Matter?

Before you throw up your hands in frustration, we should look more closely at additional findings from Belanger and Allingham's study.

Students don't understand their teachers' corrections of errors in their papers and frequently dismissed the errors their teachers marked as matters of the teachers' stylistic preferences (3).

One way to guarantee that students understand the marks you have made on their papers is to ask them to write you a letter in which they respond to each specific comment that you have made. They should indicate where they don't understand your comments. If you move around the classroom while students do this you can often clear up misunderstandings on the spot. The activity compels students to read what you have written on their papers and gives you a better return for your time invested. I don't spend any time reading these return notes but collect them for accountability.

Many teachers feel that they must mark every student error to justify the grade they assign—the lower the grade, the more red marks. According to Belanger and Allingham, the students interviewed were convinced of this universal ratio as well. Unfortunately the desired result is missing from the equation; there is no evidence that more red marks are equal to improved student writing.

The most successful comments or corrections were those referring specifically to criteria that teachers had taught in class (3).

Belanger and Allingham's research supports George Hillocks' (1986) conclusion that "The available research suggests that teaching by written comment on compositions is generally ineffective" (167).

Through their interviews the researchers found that many students responded with resentment when a teacher rewrote their sentences, "I suppose it's a better way of saying it," or "Well, that's her style but it's not mine" (3). Some students seemed genuinely hurt: "It really bothers me when someone rewrites my sentences, as if I can't write" (3). Given the amount of time teachers spend revising garbled student prose, believing all the while that they are doing the very best for their charges, this is shocking news.

In *Research on Written Composition: New Directions for Teaching* Hillocks admits, "It may be, however, that when comments are focused and tied to some aspect of instruction . . . they do increase the quality of writing" (168). Whenever I correct student papers I keep track of errors I notice cropping up in several essays and use these for minilessons on specific grammatical issues. I note where I have found particular examples in individual papers and the next day in class ask those students to share their sentence in the spirit of new common understanding and learning. My notes for the last set of tenth-grade essays I corrected looked like this:

- Flat first sentences. See Laeticia's, Roberto's, and Audra's essays.
- Mistaking "affect" and "effect." See Dylan's second paragraph, final sentence.
- Conversational expressions: "pretty much," "it's unbelievable," "story flip-flops back and forth."
- Run-on sentences. See Amy's last sentence on page 1, Max's first sentence, paragraph 3.
- Underline or italicize book titles.
- Quotations with missing page numbers. Review guidelines for citations.
- Possessives. Too many missing apostrophes particularly with plural nouns.
- Split infinitives. See Danielle's conclusion, sentence 2 and Peter's third paragraph, first sentence.

After handing back papers I spend ten to twenty minutes of class time going over these common errors and answering questions. When commenting on the next set of papers I refer to this list, reminding students that we talked about these errors.

Students searched for positive comments and lingered on the examples they found. At the same time they were quick to spot hollow praise. "Comments which were personalized seemed to give students the impression that their teachers cared about them and what they had to say" (Belanger and Allingham 2002, 8).

Belanger and Allingham's research suggests the most effective teacher comments relate the composition at hand with past writing, shared the teacher's beliefs and experiences, and validated the ideas and hypotheses of students. Students resent extensive criticism and generally ignore more than a few "well-placed, focused, and easily understood suggested changes in writing style or substance" (8). These findings support my belief that students are more likely to become more accomplished writers when they feel the teacher is on their side, cheering their successes and supporting them when they stumble. Grading student essays is a more subtle process than simple error correction.

Adrienne Mack-Kirschner, a National Board Certified Teacher and author of *Straight Talk for Today's Teachers: How to Teach So Students Learn* (2005), feels that teachers spend too much time grading, weighing, calculating, sorting, and classifying students. Her recommendation is to set standards high and then celebrate as students move toward accomplishment and mastery. In order to do this, teachers need to know their students well and respond to them as individuals. A generic "Good job!" or rubber-stamped "Excellent!" is not enough.

Responding to Student Drafts

In the light of these rather depressing conclusions about what students take away from our carefully constructed comments on final papers, it only makes sense to consider responding to students' work at an earlier stage. They are more open to suggestion and less defensive when the paper under the microscope is an early draft. The obvious problem with this suggestion is that, if we are overwhelmed with the papers we have, it is nigh impossible for us ever to read two versions of the same paper. Before I begin to describe two methods for commenting on drafts, I want to make it clear that the final versions of these student papers received only a holistic rubric score.

A method I learned from my colleague Meredith Louria was to ask students to turn in a blank cassette tape along with the first drafts of their essays. Ask students to label the tape with their name, the date, and the essay's title. (This small step for individual students will save you a great deal of time and possible confusion later.) Read the whole student essay into the tape, adding your own comments as you go. Simply hearing you struggle with their sentences can help convince some students that their prose lacks clarity. It is also easy to raise questions about those areas of the paper that are weak and to make suggestions about content as you speak informally into a tape machine. There follows an example of a tenth-grade student's draft of a term paper on Truman Capote. The italicized sentences are my comments to the student. I know that I would never have taken the time to give this kind of sentence-by-sentence response in writing. Doreen was enthusiastic about her subject and had expended considerable effort on research. It would have been a shame were her final paper to earn a poor grade for clarity. I have reproduced only the first paragraph of the report, but this will make clear the value of the method and the style of dialogue I describe.

Truman Capote: Fact Versus Fiction
by Doreen Lew

Throughout our educational lives, the differences between fiction and nonfiction are indisputable and distinct. *Is it only during our educational lives or always for readers?* The two worlds rarely coincide, and you study each type of literature separately. *I'm not sure what you mean by coincide . . . doesn't seem quite the right word here.* Yet, what happens when the two divisions come together? What becomes of a novel equally instilled with fact *and* fiction? *Are novels instilled with fiction? Or facts? Again reconsider your word choice here.* This is precisely the question that Truman Capote explored throughout his career as an author. Truman Capote, following along the paths of very few writers before him, articulately combined the skillful art

FIGURE 7–1   *Doreen Works on Her Revision*

Seems overkill to say articulately and skillful in the same sentence of fiction and narration with the objective and often ambivalent techniques of journalism, *What do you mean by ambivalent techniques of journalism? I'm lost.* while also ingeniously inter-twining almost his entire childhood and life into each and every one of his characters. *Every one? This seems a bit of an overstatement, Doreen.* To look at each work written by Capote is to see the intricate stitches that piece together his mind. Truman Capote has broken all the barriers, making his novels tales that we as readers just as much relate to as we do learn about his own life. *As you heard, I had a lot of trouble reading this last sentence. Could you try to phrase this another way?* He has not only related the opposite worlds of fact and fiction, but has made them a whole new universe together. *Hyperbolic in the extreme. Consider a less grandiose claim. It is an exciting thesis to explore, but you don't want to set out a claim that can't be defended. A whole new universe?*

My recommended method is to allow no more than ten to fifteen minutes for each draft and to use a timer to monitor your progress. Even if you don't complete work on the paper in the time allotted, your comments will give the student plenty of material to work on.

When I am responding to student drafts I ask students to identify areas in their drafts in which they feel they need assistance. I find that this is helpful both for them and for me. The cover sheet on page 94 helps students to assess their own draft's shortcomings as well as focus my comments back to them.

Fostering Improvement from One Paper to the Next

Portfolio assessment, like peer editing, was once all the rage among writing teachers. Excited by the possibility of demonstrating growth over time, English, mathematics, and social studies teachers began having their students keep portfolios. In 1992 the state of Vermont instituted a voluntary statewide portfolio project in grades 4 and 8 in both mathematics and writing with plans to expand to grade 10. Though popular among teachers, a RAND study by Daniel Koretz (1994) dampened enthusiasm for portfolio assessment. Koretz found that the wide variety of artifacts included in portfolios made them unreliable tools for measuring students and schools. As a result of this research, the use of portfolios for large-scale assessments has declined.

While portfolios may not be a suitable substitute for reliable measurement of student achievement at a state or national level, they continue to be a powerful classroom tool. Portfolios allow students to reflect on their learning. At Santa Monica High School we require all students in English classes to keep a portfolio and carry it with them from one grade level to the next. Eighth-grade teachers in our district invest considerable time having students prepare portfolios that include letters to their next year's teacher setting out what students see as their major

DRAFT COVER SHEET

Name: _____

Date: _____

Essay's working title: _____

What aspect of this draft still needs work? _____

_____

_____

_____

Where would you like me to focus my attention? Is there a section of the paper that you feel is particularly weak?

_____

_____

_____

Do you have questions about the assignment or about what you've written so far that you need answers to? Please ask away! _____

_____

_____

_____

How can I help you improve this draft? _____

_____

_____

strengths and weaknesses as writers. The process is not without its challenges. Storage of bulging folders of student work and reshuffling of portfolios from year to year is an administrative nightmare. Imagine 956 middle school portfolios arriving at your classroom door in June for distribution in September. While electronic portfolios promised a solution to the paper chase, rapid changes in technology required improved software, communication across platforms, and wide student access to computers. With the additional risk of software, hardware, or server failure, most teachers returned to trusty manila folders.

Portfolios provide a perfect opportunity for student writers to look back from where they have come and chart a course for improvement. This I find most compelling. Is there anything more discouraging than to find carefully corrected papers in the trash? I understand students' instinctive desire to destroy bad news, but poorly written papers are important artifacts for documenting progress. When I hand back student papers I also pass out students' portfolios and have students log each addition to their folder. The purpose of this method is to ensure that students, not I, compile the portfolios. Students return their folders—in alphabetical order—to a banker's box for their class. On back-to-school night in the fall and open house in the spring these boxes are on display for parents to peruse. The spirit of glasnost prevails.

Toward the end of each semester I ask students to read through the work they have completed over the past few months and write a letter to themselves reflecting on their progress or lack thereof. You will notice in both Cara and Gennady's missives that they have appropriated language from my comments on their essays. Cara is a model student: hardworking, cheerful, and compliant. Her letter was written in January of her sophomore year.

Dear Cara,
You have been doing well on your essays so far this year. My advice to you, though, is to work on clarifying your points. You have good ideas, but your main weakness is expressing those ideas thoughtfully and insightfully. Although only the first semester has passed, you have continued to improve. Make sure that when you read the literature you take very careful notes so that you can pick the best quotations and thoroughly analyze them.

Keep up the good work, and don't be afraid to mix things up a bit when dealing with the essay structure. As your quirky yet intelligent eighth grade English teacher put it, "variety is the spice of life!"

Sincerely,
Cara Safon

Gennady is in the same class. An instinctive mathematician and an excellent reader, he rarely takes time for revision. His work was often turned in late and in somewhat shabby condition. This letter is a perfect example of inadequate attention. Gennady describes a few of his shortcomings and then proceeds to make the very errors he identifies. Notice how he has lifted teacher phrases like "lack of analysis" and "plot-driven areas" from my comments.

Dear Gennady,
I know if you spend the time to read the essays over before turning them in you will be able to find the minner errors. You should also pay attention and be on the look out for run on sentences. If you read the essay over you will also be able to detect lack of analysis, unclear points, and plot driven areas. While reading remember to mark up the book it makes it easier to find points in the story for essays and so forth.

Your friend,
Gennady Tsarinsky

Portfolios help transfer responsibility for improvement from the teacher to the student. They also provide an invaluable record of student work for teachers' conferences with parents. Conversations about grades and student achievement are much more productive when we have essays at hand.

Husbanding Your Strength

Given that students need to write much more than you can possibly read, you are obliged to be selective about what student work you choose to read. Some teachers require students to write three essays and then tell the class that any one of the three, chosen at random, will be graded. Others have students write a bouquet of papers and let the student choose the best essay to submit for assessment. Neither of these methods has worked well for me. I don't feel it is fair to have students take a paper to completion without receiving a response from me. I also think it is unrealistic to expect students to put in their best effort when they know they have the option of discarding two out of three papers.

My solution is to read every essay but hardly anything else students write. Again, I am not suggesting that this is paragon pedagogy or what I would do under closer-to-ideal conditions where I taught fewer students. I do it to survive. For example, when assessing vocabulary I never ask students to write meaning-laden sentences or stories using the vocabulary words. A matching quiz is much easier to grade and doesn't eat into the time I have set aside for grading papers.

I often ask students to write in class as preparation for a discussion but rarely more than glance at these papers. Consider this: if you collect 150 papers and spend even one minute on each—an optimistic estimate given the time it takes to record a grade, it will take an hour and a half to get through the stack. Abandoning writing-to-learn as a strategy is a poor solution to the problem. Writing is a powerful tool for developing ideas. A few minutes alone with a question helps students garner their thoughts and results in increased class participation. It also deepens the quality of student responses. For example, today I asked my twelfth-grade students who had just finished reading Part 1 of *Crime and Punishment* to write on the following subject as a preparation for class discussion:

Lost in Translation

Prestuplenie is the Russian word for "crime." It comes from *pre* meaning "across" or "trans-" and *stuplenie* "a stepping." It is similar to the English word "transgression." Thus the Russian concept of crime is a "stepping across" some barrier. Dostoevsky plays on this concept through the novel, but it is lost in translation. Reflect on this definition of "crime." What barriers has Raskolnikov stepped across?

I told students that we would be writing for five minutes, but they appeared to apply themselves so I let them write longer. I then called on a student, one who was not normally the first to raise her hand with an answer, to talk about what she thought. The purpose of this method is not to have students read what they have written but rather to use what they have written to help them be more articulate. As you can see from the two samples of written responses below, their replies are thoughtful without being examples of fine writing.

Student Responses

Raskolnikov has "stepped across" an invisible line, and now, just like Kurtz in *Heart of Darkness*, lives on the dark side. There is never any way he can go back to his old life. He is now stuck in this new world. He has seen things no normal man has ever seen. He has opened up the evil/dark side of him. It's exciting and he wants to stay in touch with this side. He has unleashed the monster.
—*Danielle Farzam*

Raskolnikov crosses the barrier of right and wrong. He's committing a murder to "right" things, but immorality cannot give birth to morality. Killing anybody for almost any reason is a barrier not to be crossed and to proceed to kill Lizaveta takes this a step further and instead of a smaller crime or smaller step across a barrier, it's a great step in immorality.
—*Rebecca Edwards*

We had a lively class discussion that was richer for the time spent thinking with pen in hand. I collected the papers at the end of the period—students seem to feel cheated if I don't—and did nothing further with them. I needed to save my eyes for the essays they would be turning in two days later.

Ten Tips for Handling the Paper Load

1. **Do it now**. The shorter the lag time between your receipt, grading, and return of students' papers, the more likely students are to care about their performance. Think of it this way. You are going to spend the same number of minutes reading a set of papers whether you spread it out over two weeks or put your

head down and finish them in a day or two. My advice is to do it now. This might mean staggering due dates for papers for your various classes or scheduling papers to come in over a weekend but, whatever your plan, avoid letting a stack of essays age and gather dust. It isn't healthy for you to feel guilty all the time.

2. **Set aside extended periods of time for grading.** Reading essays between classes is inefficient. Don't drive yourself crazy hoping to read one here and read another there. Along with causing you to reread whole portions of a paper when interrupted, the consistency of your scoring will suffer.

3. **Use a timer.** If you know or suspect that you are taking too much time deliberating over student papers, set a timer. Ten minutes should be the absolute maximum you spend on a three-page paper. Try to build up your speed so that you are able to complete the reading of and commenting on a paper in approximately eight minutes.

4. **Stretch between each paper.** I used to develop a series of aches and pains after grading a set of papers until I realized that I hadn't moved for an hour and that I desperately needed to stretch. Do some neck rolls and hand shaking. Rotate your shoulders. If you feel like indulging yourself, luxuriate in a massage after finishing that stack of term papers.

5. **Investigate computer scoring.** Find out if your school has access to computerized scoring resources. Experiment with having one class submit their papers for electronic evaluation. Consider this as a way of helping you offer students additional writing practice.

6. **Use a rubric.** Along with providing greater scoring transparency for students, rubrics can help you assess papers with greater accuracy. If you are overwhelmed by the number of student papers you need to grade, give yourself permission to score a set of essays holistically. Staple a copy of the rubric you used for evaluation to every student paper.

7. **Avoid reading papers when you are exhausted.** It is easy to grow bitter about teaching English when you push yourself past endurance. I try to take some exercise when I return home

from school, have dinner, and then sit down to a marathon session with student papers. If I am overtired or harried, the essays seem worse than they actually are. All I can see are the errors.

8. **No interruptions.** When you are reading papers the temptation is to celebrate when the phone or doorbell rings. Any excuse suffices to look up from student scribbling. Any reason to walk away from your desk. To the extent possible—and I recognize that this won't work with small babies—try to have others in your household handle interruptions so that you can work in peace and without interruption. Don't answer the phone. Concentration is the key to moving through a set of papers efficiently.

9. **Make sure your students read your comments.** You invest time and effort into grading student papers. To ensure a return for that investment, on the day you hand back papers structure a lesson that requires students to process what you have written and commit themselves to improving their composition skills.

10. **Save all student papers.** Have students keep a portfolio of their graded essays. Periodically invite students to reread these pieces and consider their progress as writers. At the end of the academic year ask students to choose a paper they are particularly proud of and to write a reflective essay exploring why this piece seemed to work so well.

EIGHT

One Hand for the Ship
One Hand for Yourself

"One hand for the ship, one hand for yourself" is an old watchword in the U.S. Navy that offers advice to sailors about to clamber up a ship's rigging. If sailors climb to their stations and only hang on for dear life, no work is done. If they don't hold on, they are lost. The metaphor is equally apt for the teaching profession. When individuals only take care of themselves, the work of the ship—or society—suffers. But if individuals don't save one hand for themselves, they will founder.

Teachers of writing should consider this maritime message. Too many young teachers give both hands to the job, sacrificing their personal lives and even their health to the demands of their classroom: designing lessons, putting up bulletin boards, calling parents, staying late, arriving early, and grading papers long into the night. As a result, the best and the brightest often decide they want a less restrictive life and leave the profession. This is not to say that only inferior specimens remain—remember, this is my thirty-first year in the classroom. Yet I, too, considered applying to law school after four years of teaching. I loved my work with middle school students but had little professional contact with anyone outside Lincoln Junior High School. My best friend, whom I met while we were working on our teaching credentials, was going to law school and I thought I might as well go, too. It is frightening to consider how decisions that change our lives are made.

I took the LSAT, was accepted at several law schools, and began working out the financial implications. I felt law school might be a way to do something for myself, allowing me to shackle my hand to a line that didn't lead back only to my students. Fortunately, two things happened. Halfway up a Swiss mountain, when I was able to look from a distance at the prospect of a career in the legal profession, my husband asked two pointed questions.

"Do you really want to be a lawyer?"

"No."

"Then why do you want to go to law school?" I had no answer. The second fortunate event happened when I accepted an invitation to attend a summer California Writing Project institute at UCLA and became involved with the National Writing Project. Instead of reaching outside education to broaden my horizons, I was introduced to and embraced a wider professional community.

To this day I feel guilty about the lack of professional capital I brought to that Writing Project community. My fellow participants were experts in the field, grappling with issues of rhetoric and composition. I wasn't entirely sure what "rhetoric" was and still split infinitives. Ruth Mitchell, Dick Dodge, Rae Jean Williams, Diane Dawson, Genee Gossard, and others never made me feel stupid, however. They welcomed me into their world where sharing ideas for improving writing instruction was a way of life. No one person had all the answers. We heard from experts like Richard Lanham and worked through each other's writing lessons. Over the course of those five weeks I learned pedagogical strategies that would help me retain my balance on the hire-wire act of classroom teaching. I also experienced the power of professional friendships.

Richard Ingersoll's (2003) research report "Is There Really a Teacher Shortage?" cites statistics on teacher attrition that demonstrate that during the first five years of teaching 40–50 percent of new teachers leave the profession. His implications for policy are clear:

> In short, the data suggest that school staffing problems are rooted in the way schools are organized and the way the teaching occupation is treated and that lasting improvements in the quality and quantity of the teaching workforce will require improvements in the quality of the teaching job. (20)

The problem is not that too few teachers are entering the profession or that too many teachers are retiring. Individuals with other options choose to leave teaching because they are unhappy with their teaching lives. If schools hope to retain promising young teachers—the kind who will go on to be future leaders in the profession—they need to help one another figure out how to maintain "one hand for the ship, one hand for yourself." Ingersoll's research concluded that many of the teachers leaving the classroom had little or no mentoring (24). Whether or not formal mentor programs are in place at a school, experienced teachers need to reach out to the new teachers around them not only with the offer of their files but also with a hand.

- Talk without shame about how you manage to handle the paper load.
- Offer paper-grading sessions where teachers work together.
- Publicize anchor papers so teachers feel comfortable about their grading standards.
- Urge schools to use funding to reduce class size in writing classes.
- Channel PTSA and other supplemental funding sources to tutoring and outside readers rather than field trips.

Effective teachers know how to give their students a full hand of help. They also know that preserving their second hand for themselves makes for a happier, healthier, better-balanced life. The biggest problem facing American education is not the shortage of teachers but rather the shortage of good teachers. Schools don't need more martyrs. They need professionals who can survive and thrive in a challenging job. I hope this book will help you do so and remember, "One hand for the ship, one hand for yourself."

~

Works Cited

—

BELANGER, JOE, AND PHILIP V. ALLINGHAM. 2002. Using "Think Aloud" Methods to Investigate the Processes Secondary School Students Use to Respond to Their Teachers' Comments on Their Written Work. Technical Report. The University of British Columbia: www.lerc.educ.ubc.ca/fac/belanger/thinkaloud.htm.

CALIFORNIA DEPARTMENT OF EDUCATION. 1997. *English-Language Arts Content Standards for California Public Schools*. Sacramento: California Department of Education.

CHEVILLE, JULIE. 2004. "Automated Scoring Technologies and the Rising Influence of Error." *English Journal* 93 (4): 47–51.

DELPIT, LISA. 1995. *Other People's Children*. New York: The New Press.

EDUCATIONAL TESTING SERVICE. Praxis II. www.ets.org/praxis/prxtest.html.

FOLTZ, P. W., KINTSCH, W., AND T. K. LANDAUER. 1998. "The Measurement of Textual Coherence with Latent Semantic Analysis." *Discourse Processes* 25 (2, 3): 285–307.

HILLOCKS, GEORGE. 1986. *Research on Written Composition: New Directions for Teaching*. Urbana, IL: NCRE/ERIC Clearinghouse.

INGERSOLL, RICHARD M. 2003. "Is There Really a Teacher Shortage?" Research report by Center for the Study of Teaching and Policy and The Consortium for Policy Research in Education. September.

JAGO, CAROL. 2000. *With Rigor for All: Teaching the Classics to Contemporary Students*. Portsmouth, NH: Heinemann.

———. 2002. *Cohesive Writing: Why Concept Is Not Enough.* Portsmouth, NH: Heinemann.

KORETZ, DANIEL. 1994. *Can Portfolios Assess Student Performance and Influence Instruction? The 1991–92 Vermont Experience.* RAND/RP-259.

MACK-KIRSCHNER, ADRIENNE. 2005. *Straight Talk for Today's Teachers: How to Teach So Students Learn.* Portsmouth, NH: Heinemann.

MANZO, KATHLEEN KENNEDY. 2003. Essay Grading Goes Digital, Technology Counts 2003 report. *Education Week* on the Web. http://counts.edweek.org/sreports/tc03/article.cfm?slug=35 essays.h22.

McGRATH, CHARLES. 2004. "Writing to the Test." Education Life, *New York Times.* November 7, p. 27.

MURRAY, BRIDGET. 1998. The Latest Techno Tool: Essay-Grading Computers. *The American Psychological Association Monitor.* http://apa.org/monitor/aug98/grade.html.

NATIONAL ASSESSMENT OF EDUCATIONAL PROGRESS IN WRITING WEBSITE. http://nces.ed.gov/nationsreportcard/itmrls/qtab.asp

NATIONAL COMMISSION ON TEACHING AND AMERICA'S FUTURE. 2003. *No Dream Denied, A Pledge to America's Children: Summary Report.* Washington, D.C.

NATIONAL COMMISSION ON WRITING IN AMERICA'S SCHOOLS AND COLLEGES. 2003. *The Neglected "R."* New York: The College Board. April.

OAKI, NAOMI. 2004. Harshness of Red Marks Has Students Seeing Purple. *Boston Globe*, August 24, 2004. www.boston.com/news/education/k_12/articles/2004/08/23/harshness_of_red_marks_has_students_seeing_purple/.

PAGE, E. B., J. P. POGGIO, AND T. Z. KEITH. 1997. Computer Analysis of Student Essays: Finding Trait Differences in the Student Profile. AERA/NCME Symposium on Grading Essays by Computer. http://pareonline.net/getvn.asp?v=7&n=26.

PUBLIC AGENDA. 1997. Getting By: What American Teenagers Really Think About Their Schools. www.shearonforschools.com/Getting%20By.htm.

RILKE, RAINER MARIA. 1962. *Letters to a Young Poet.* New York: W.W. Norton.

RODRIGUEZ, RICHARD. 1983. *Hunger of Memory: The Education of Richard Rodriguez.* New York: Bantam Press.

WORKS CITED

ROSE, MIKE. 1999. *Lives on the Boundary: The Struggles and Achievements of America's Underprepared*. New York: Touchstone.

THE AMERICAN DIPLOMA PROJECT. 2004. *Ready or Not: Creating a High School Diploma That Counts*. The American Diploma Project, Washington D.C.: Achieve.

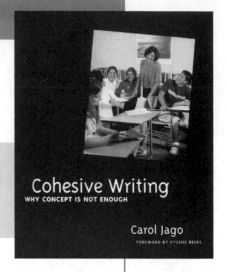